PREPARING TO TEACH IN ELEMENTARY CLASSROOMS

PREPARING TO TEACH IN ELEMENTARY CLASSROOMS

AN INTRODUCTION TO BECOMING AN EFFECTIVE CHILDHOOD EDUCATOR

First Edition

Kimberly Rombach, Ph.D.

cognella®

SAN DIEGO

Bassim Hamadeh, CEO and Publisher
John Remington, Executive Editor
Carrie Baarns, Manager, Revisions and Author Care
Gem Rabanera, Senior Project Editor
Jordan Krikorian, Editorial Assistant
Celeste Paed, Production Editor
Kim Scott, Graphic Design Assistant
JoHannah McDonald, Licensing Coordinator
Natalie Piccotti, Director of Marketing
Kassie Graves, Senior Vice President, Editorial
Jamie Giganti, Director of Academic Publishing

Cover image: Copyright © 2015 Depositphotos/Rawpixel.

Printed in the United States of America.

320 South Cedros Ave., Ste. 400, Solana Beach, CA 92075

DEDICATION

To my mom and dad, Kathy and Marty, who taught me to always do my best and to find the best in every situation. To my siblings, JoAnn, Mike, and Don, for always supporting me. To my children, Katie and Joey, who have become my unexpected and wonderful teachers of life, love, and family. To my many friends who were early readers of this book and encouraged me to share what I have learned and experienced. To my former colleagues and students at Walberta Park School, whose memories have a very special place in my heart and to my colleagues and preservice teachers at SUNY Cortland, who always give me hope in tomorrow's classrooms. I thank all of you for your continued love and support that inspires me every day.

CONTENTS

INTRODUCTION

Hello future teacher! I am excited that you want to become a teacher! We need more great teachers in the world, and I hope you will become one of them. When I've talked with educators, most have said it's not easy to become a great teacher. In fact, they often say it takes years of hard work and dedication to become truly accomplished in our profession. What can be done to help you to become prepared now? I believe it is important for future teachers like yourself to know what matters most when teaching so that you will be well prepared to help all students reach their fullest potential.

Years ago, I was introduced to the idea of a *touchstone*, and I've chosen to use it as an important metaphor for us as you read this book. Historically, a touchstone was a hard, black stone used to test for gold. When ordinary metals were struck across the touchstone, no marks were left behind. When gold was rubbed across it, however, it would leave a streak, revealing its presence. Since gold is a metal with great value, it has been used symbolically to identify high standards and excellence. Blending the early practice of identifying gold with the symbolism it evokes, this text, *Preparing to Teach in Elementary Classrooms*, introduces the term *touchstone* to establish universal reference points that you can use as benchmarks for your own teaching.

To help you make connections from the research to your own teaching, I've written a collection of personal letters to you and have included them in each chapter. The letters offer insights into what the research is really saying. They provide real stories from classrooms and explain how to use the research to inform your own teaching. Each chapter also includes a chart that includes, quite simply, what to do and what not to do when teaching. Chapters end with discussion prompts to use as a guide for collaborative dialogue in class or in study groups.

Preparing to Teach in Elementary Classrooms has been organized into six parts. Part 1, "Who We Are," includes information about the importance of understanding that teachers' ideas, opinions, and perspectives about students matter. It asks you to consider who you are now and who you will be for your future students. What expectations will you have of them? In what ways will you portray your sense of care for their learning? Answers to these questions will impact your future students' success in your class, and the first three chapters of this book will illuminate this for you.

No students are alike. Each has their own unique abilities, personalities, and traits that they bring into their classrooms every day. Part 2, "Who We Teach," includes three chapters that portray ways students are uniquely diverse and how you, as an emerging teacher, can work toward developing knowledge and skills to be responsive to your future students' cultures, to their strengths and needs, and to who they are individually and socially.

No two schools are the same. Someday, you may teach in a public, private, charter, or magnet school. Each offers their own opportunities for students and families. Part 3, "Where We Teach," offers insight into different types of schools and provides information about the importance of understanding the tone and climate of each and the role you will someday have with contributing to it. Think back to an elementary school you attended. What feelings did you have when you were in your school? What do you think contributed to your feelings? Answers to these questions begin to describe a school's climate, and the two chapters in this section portray factors that contribute to creating a positive, effective learning environment for students you will someday teach.

All teachers are different, and each have their own way of teaching. Research reveals, however, that how teachers teach can either promote or at times hinder student learning. What approaches make a difference when promoting student learning? Part 4, "How We Teach," explains the importance of using strengths-based, whole-child approaches when teaching. It explains lesson planning, student engagement, and classroom behavior and, perhaps most important, describes how and why these three elements are closely related.

Elementary school teachers are subject matter experts. They are expected to know both what and how to teach in each content area, including literacy, math, science, and social studies. Part 5, "What We Teach," describes teaching a different type of content that will promote students' learning in each of these areas. Chapter 12 incudes information about how to promote a classroom that is socially just, what content is associated with it, and ways to create a classroom community in which all students' voices matter and all students have every opportunity to reach their greatest potential. Chapter 13 is about how you can help your future students learn about their social and emotional interactions with others and why it matters to be highly conscious of it.

The last part of this book, Part 6, "Why We Teach," describes the importance of recognizing the unique position you will someday have as a potential advocate for your future students. What does advocacy mean to you? In what ways would students need a committed advocate on their side? How can teachers be advocates for their students? Questions such as these are explored in the last two chapters, and you will be guided to inquire about ways you can advocate for students' needs to promote their development. The last chapter offers insight into how you can contribute to the teaching profession. The world needs teachers who are committed to creating classrooms and schools where all students thrive. The teaching profession needs teachers who will do their absolute best to make that happen. I hope you are up for the challenge and that this book will guide you along the way.

PART 1

Who We Are

■ CHAPTER 1

GETTING READY

Dear aspiring teachers everywhere,

I know that you are probably thinking that you have plenty of time to learn how to teach, but the truth is that not long from now you'll be setting foot into your first classroom and, before entering it, we need you to work hard to become the very best teacher you can be. I hope your students say that YOU were the best teacher they ever had. Are you ready? Our profession will ask much of you, and I hope that you are up for the challenge.

With warm regards,

K.

I am so excited that you want to become a teacher! You are entering a challenging yet extremely rewarding profession because you will have the opportunity to make a profound and lasting impact on your students' lives. Every day you will be able to choose the type of teacher you want to be. It's important for you to realize that right from the start, what you say, what you do, and how you do it, will irrationally, unexpectedly, and unknowingly impact your students' lives. Perhaps you have been preparing to become a teacher for a long time, or maybe you will be entering our profession soon after you decided to become a teacher. Whichever the case, I hope that you will enter with a sense of passion and care for what you choose to do and how you choose to do it. That choice will be yours to make every single day.

Sometimes I think teachers believe their experiences are uniquely their own, but as I've taught longer, I've come to realize that teachers all over the world share many universal experiences. Regardless of classroom, school, or community, you will likely share a collection of experiences with other teachers. You see, at some point in your career, you will inevitably experience a struggling student's light bulb moment, and you will likely experience a student's unpredictable outburst that will shed light on a troubled personal life. Each experience in its own way can and probably will elicit a sense of teaching being worthwhile for you. Also like all teachers, at some point you will experience the need to carry out swift, on-the-spot decision-making. Many in the field of education suggest that teachers make nearly 1,500 decisions every single day and some say that is a low estimate (Klein, 2021). Therefore, it is important for you to develop a strong knowledge base to inform and guide the decision-making you will do.

Perhaps one of the most important decisions that I would like to ask you to make is to consciously decide, unequivocally, what kind of teacher you want to be. I ask this of you because you will soon carry the enormous responsibility of shaping students' lives. Consider this short quote from a six-year-old: "My teacher thought I was smarter than I am—so I was." Wow! This teacher's belief about one child actually caused his perception of himself (his reality) to change. She literally changed who he saw himself to be. It is troubling to think what might have happened if the teacher saw this student as anything less than what she did! You have probably already experienced some of the influences teachers have had on your own life. Perhaps there were times when you may have felt invisible around a teacher or perhaps a teacher helped you believe in yourself. A teacher's influence is far more powerful than you might have previously considered.

I'd like to tell you a story about a woman named Ms. Lenore Jacobson who was a principal at Spruce Elementary School in South San Francisco, California, in the 1960s. Ms. Jacobson perceived that her teachers' beliefs about their students might influence their outcomes so she invited a psychologist, Dr. Robert Rosenthal, to carry out a study in her school. Together, they inquired into ways that teachers' beliefs may unconsciously influence students' outcomes. At the beginning of their study, they provided a false intelligence test to students, told the teachers that they had graded it and the test scores identified students who would become the "academic bloomers," which, based on their test results, meant that they would begin to outperform their classmates. The study was designed so the teachers did not know the "academic bloomers" were randomly selected; they were no different than their classmates. Ms. Jacobson and Dr. Rosenthal found that, in time, teachers actually began to treat students who were referred to as the "academic bloomers" differently than their peers, and a year later, the "academic bloomers" showed greater academic gains than the other students. Therefore, Jacobson and Rosenthal concluded that since teachers expected the "academic bloomers" to have greater academic success, they did. Teachers' positive expectations had impacted how their students behaved, how others treated them, and subsequently, the outcomes they achieved (Rosenthal & Jacobson, 1968). The idea that teachers' expectations will affect their students' performance has been referred to as the Pygmalion effect. Although some criticism has emerged regarding the study's design, I think you would find it interesting to know that additional educational studies completed afterward portray very similar findings: teachers' expectations can and will impact their students' outcomes (Rosenthal & Babad, 1985).

Rosenthal and Jacobson explained that four factors led to this self-fulfilling prophecy that can inform teaching practices. The first is that there is a climate factor which means that teachers often create warmer, kinder individual climates (i.e., interactions) with students they perceive to be higher achievers, and this act has been found to positively influence students' academic outcomes. It is important for teachers to apply this finding to their own teaching. So, it is essential that all teachers use care with their verbal and nonverbal communication to ensure that each student feels appreciated and valued. The second factor Rosenthal described was an input factor, which simply means that teachers often teach more content to students they perceive as higher achievers. So, as a teacher, it will be important for you to consciously attend to this potential effect by providing multiple opportunities to extend all students' learning by introducing new, additional content when possible. Doing so can positively influence all students' academic outcomes. The third factor is the response opportunity factor, which refers to the way that teachers provide students they perceive to be higher achievers with more response time when answering questions. Therefore, when you are teaching, be sure to provide all students with similar opportunities to respond and express answers in multiple ways. The last factor is the feedback factor, which refers to the higher quality and greater quantity of feedback that teachers give students they perceive to be higher achieving than others. As such, in your classroom, be sure to provide steady and specific feedback to all students (Rosenthal & Jacobson, 1968; Rosenthal & Rubin, 1978).

I have highlighted Rosenthal and Jacobson's findings to identify your first, and perhaps most important touchstone for successful teaching: **Your expectations will affect your students' outcomes**.

Hello again,

One summer before school began, a mother of one of my future students sent me a letter to ask to meet with me. I phoned her right away and set up a time to get together at the school. After a short welcome, she said, "I wanted to meet to ask something of you." She continued, "I am worried that you won't see the full potential in my daughter. I want her to become a reader by the end of the year." I said, "That's a goal that I have of all students." And she replied, "No, I don't mean a goal; I want you to believe that she can do it from the start." Through the rest of our conversation, I came to find out that Lydia had Down syndrome and very limited verbal expression. Her mother repeated, "Do you believe that she can become a reader?" I said, "Sure I do." Without knowing it, Lydia's mom brought this first touchstone to life for me. You see, in her own way, Lydia's mom was asking me to ensure that my beliefs and my communication with Lydia would convey—without reservation—that she would read. Her inquiry gave way to questioning my own assumptions about children with Down syndrome which, if I hadn't consciously and carefully thought about it, might have limited Lydia's outcomes. And guess what? By the end of the year, Lydia became a strong reader!

Yours truly,

K.

Descriptions help our ideas become clearer. Sometimes we describe things by their characteristics, and other times we gain clarity through examples. I believe that you will understand the touchstones in this text in a more comprehensive way by also having dialectic descriptions of each. Dialectic descriptions provide a way to understand the features of a concept by contrasting their attributes with their opposites. In other words, dialectic descriptions can provide insight into what something is by identifying what it is not. Therefore, I have included dialectic descriptions at the end of each chapter in this book to identify what to what to do and what not to do when implementing touchstones into your classroom.

TOUCHSTONE FOR TEACHING: YOUR EXPECTATIONS WILL AFFECT YOUR STUDENTS' OUTCOMES

What to Do	What Not to Do
Look for the best in every student. It's the best place to start.	Don't have fixed beliefs about students' aptitude. It will not help them succeed.
Provide steady and specific feedback to everyone. Feedback provides direction for goal setting.	Don't reply more often to some students than others. Balance matters.
Let all students know you care. Care is the grandest student motivator.	Be careful not to favor some students over others. Students will notice and it won't help.
Express positive expectations for all students. They deserve it.	Don't expect that some students will underperform compared to others. It can set students up for failure.
Remember, if you have higher expectations, your students will have higher outcomes.	Don't limit your expectations of students. Doing so will influence your students to have lower outcomes.

Caring Matters

Research reveals that when students are asked to describe teachers who made a difference in their lives, they initially and often describe traits associated with care. The notion of care is often thought of as a soft skill because it resides in what we call the affective domain and, as such, orients our focus on feelings and emotions. This initially seems contradictory to our notion of learning, which resides in the cognitive (thinking) domain. It is important for future teachers to know that students' affective domain (i.e., feelings) can substantially enhance or interrupt learning. According to Marzano (1992), effective teachers are able to skillfully and consciously participate in the development of students' attitudes and perceptions about learning. So you as an aspiring teacher may ask, how would I do that? We have a substantial literature base that suggests teachers' aptitude with developing genuinely caring teacher-to-student relationships is one of the most important factors contributing to students' positive feelings about school and their learning and, subsequently, their outcomes. To understand this more, I would like to introduce you to the important work of Nel Noddings.

Noddings focuses on the importance of teachers developing caring relationships with students and suggests that while we often hear that "all teachers care," this is not always true (Noddings, 2005). She says that we all can probably remember teachers who were unkind and said hurtful comments to us or to our classmates. Although the unkind teachers may have cared about the act of teaching, they likely fell short on establishing caring, trusting relationships with their students (Noddings, 2005). Noddings distinguishes two different forms of care by identifying one as a virtuous form that refers to teachers showing concern for and interest in students' educational goals and achievement and another as a relational form of care that focuses on teachers' interpersonal interactions with students, including listening and conversing to purposefully foster students' feelings of value and importance. Noddings suggests that teachers' relational care needs to be the framework for pedagogy, the context of our teaching.

Noddings's call for developing a sense of relational care is supported by those who study relational pedagogy, which encourages teachers to begin and sustain interpersonal interactions with students to portray feelings of liking, trust, and respect. Stronge reports that research on student learning has found that students who have caring relationships with teachers experience far greater academic successes than those who don't (Zakrzewski, 2012). Our literature on teaching includes findings from hundreds of studies that reveal similar findings and, as such, provide us with the second touchstone: **Your relational care will nurture students' success**.

To be honest, developing a genuine sense of care for individual students is not always easy to do. That's because it requires a one-teacher-to-one-student connection within a classroom context that is usually designed as a one-teacher-to-many-students experience. For that reason, you will probably find it challenging to connect personally with each student because so much of your school day will be about relating to youth collectively. This will also require you to develop a sense of trust with your students so that they come to feel comfortable interacting with you.

Greetings again, future teachers,

I'd like to tell you that I knew all of this when I first started teaching, but I didn't.

When I began, my focus was more on what to teach than on who I was teaching. I thought a lot, almost exclusively, about planning interesting activities to introduce new content and to make learning "fun." As I taught, my lessons seemed to flow one into the other and my classroom seemed to hum along smoothly so I thought I was being successful as a teacher. However, my way of doing things came crashing down on me the moment David walked into my classroom. As a kindergartner, David was diagnosed with cancer, and while undergoing surgery to remove a tumor, he had a stroke that affected the use of the right side of his body. He entered my classroom the following year with a smile, and as he walked to his desk, he pulled a trash can up alongside him because he was nauseous from frequent chemotherapy. While I had my own internal struggles with understanding his parents' desire to keep him in school, I had no other choice than to think about David's needs first, before the curriculum. Throughout that year, I asked David about his thoughts and feelings about school and our classroom. I listened and made changes to my planning and teaching and developed an understanding of the need to know—to really know—who my students were as individuals. Through this experience, I came to understand the focus that Noddings suggests—to realize the impact of my relational care on students' outcomes. As I got to know David and his needs, the individual connections I had with him and his classmates shifted to the heart of my work. I learned to think of them first, then the curriculum. As a future teacher, I believe it will be important for you to consciously have your students as the central focus of your teaching. This touchstone about relational care can remind you that each of your students will have an experience with you that is uniquely their own, and you will need to find ways to genuinely develop a true sense of care with each of them. Is there a way that you can create a sense of care so strong that when each student leaves your classroom, each will believe they mattered most to you?

warmly,

K.

I hope that you teach with a deep sense of care for all students and for their learning. I also hope that you have a deep sense of care for our profession as well. While the idea of relational care can inform who you are in a classroom, it is also important to consider the care that you will have for our teaching profession.

We do not often think of an inheritance factor when we enter the teaching profession because we assume that our own personal traits are those that will shape us as teachers. While this is true, other preexisting factors will contribute to you becoming a professional as well. Each school has its own culture and community in which you will work. Those particular traits will in some way inform who you become as an emerging professional. Some schools have particular cultures that are known to feel warmer than others; some are more student centered, while others are more outcomes driven. So, while you will of course bring a lot of "you" to our profession, it is important to recognize that upon entering, you will inherit some of our profession's attributes as well.

When you become a teacher, you will undoubtedly find others who will have a love of learning and a passion for inspiring students, too. You will find teachers who are dedicated to their work and to serving their communities. Recent research suggests, however, that there is a growing, unprecedented criticism toward our profession that has caused veteran, novice, and aspiring teachers to feel discouraged and dispassionate about our educational system.

Once again, hello,

I didn't think that I'd be in touch again so soon, but I want to let you know right up front that this is a very challenging time for you to be entering our profession. You will soon come to realize (if you haven't already) that you will need to overcome loads of criticism about teaching; to be successful, you will need to develop a strong and steady courageous resilience against it. You see, the difficulty is that the critics of teaching now reside both within and outside of our own profession. Despite this, do you think that you can enter and stay in the teaching profession and have deep care and devotion to it?

With hope,

K.

Our profession has grown restless. Nearly half of those who will begin a teaching career quit within the first 5 years. Our research on teacher retention has identified that teachers leave the profession not because they were unprepared to teach, but due to job dissatisfaction. Research on teachers who stay report that far too many say they have acquired apathy toward teaching that can't be overcome. With nearly 1.5 million retiring soon, new teachers like you will have the opportunity to renew our teaching workforce. I hope that you will uphold and advocate for our collective work and our profession. Just as research suggests that you should have high expectations of your students, I hope that you have high expectations of yourself—to care about the way you portray yourself as a professional so you can proactively contribute to the restitution and revitalization of teaching.

The first two touchstones can offer you a wonderful starting place as a teacher. It is important you know that the expectations you have of your students and the relational care you portray will affect their academic outcomes. Who you choose to become as a teacher can and will impact our teaching profession. I encourage you to think about ways to contribute to our profession by caring enough to become the best teacher you can be in all you will do.

TOUCHSTONE FOR TEACHING: YOUR RELATIONAL CARE WILL NURTURE STUDENTS' SUCCESS

What to Do	What Not to Do
Listen to students' stories. They have important ideas to share.	Don't pretend to listen to students. They will know you are pretending.
Know what and who students care about. It will help you relate to them personally.	Don't give more attention to some students than others; balancing your attention among all students matters.
Know students' worries. It provides insight into their lives.	Be careful not to use put-downs for any reason. It will not help.
Tell students they are valued. It will help them to feel individually worthwhile.	Don't use sarcasm or teasing to try to make connections with students. It won't work.
Communicate often with students to convey that their lives matter to you.	Don't communicate negatively about students anywhere with anyone. It is the wrong focus to have.

Questions for Discussion and Reflection

▪ Think back to your own schooling experiences. Can you recall a teacher who made a difference in your life? What characteristics and traits did that teacher have?

▪ This chapter distinguished the difference between two types of care teachers may portray when interacting with students. Explore this further by identifying what teachers would say and do when portraying a sense of virtuous care and relational care. In what ways might the two approaches affect students differently?

▪ One of the scenarios in this chapter mentioned some of the struggles associated with teaching David, a first grader with cancer, and the teacher's planning. Why would it be important to think about *who* you teach before thinking about *what* you teach? This implies a student-first approach. What might this approach look like when teachers plan lessons?

Fig. 1.1. Copyright © 2012 Depositphotos/Pressmaster.

CHAPTER 2

ENGAGING FAMILIES AND CAREGIVERS AS PARTNERS

I t probably comes as no surprise to you that students with parents who are *involved* with their education earn higher grades and develop stronger social skills than those without such parental support (Epstein, 1991). Research findings in this area are so significant that we have federal policies requiring schools and teachers to provide educational experiences that engage parents in students' educational experiences.

Our overarching national education law, the Elementary and Secondary Education Act, reauthorized in 2002 as No Child Left Behind (NCLB) and again in 2015 as Every Student Succeeds Act (ESSA), requires school districts to write family engagement policies in collaboration with parents, a plan to essentially implement meaningful parent/family school activities and to assess these efforts with an annual evaluation of the policy. One component of the family engagement policy requires Title 1 schools (those schools that serve at least 40% of children from low-income families) to include a collaboratively developed School-Parent Compact that describes how "parents, the entire school staff, and students will share the responsibility for improved student academic achievement and the means by which *the school and parents will build and develop a partnership* to help students achieve the State's high standards" (ESSA, 2015). Perhaps you are thinking that this is something that is already happening in schools or perhaps you are thinking that this is something that teachers support. If so, think again. While teachers and parents often realize the need for each other to be key players in students' education, the act of them coming together as partners is still far from being common in today's schools. For years, the media has, at times, represented tensions between teachers and parents as an unfortunate "blame game" where some parents blame teachers for failing their students and some teachers blame parents for not being more involved. Throughout time, blaming and criticizing has placed these two groups at odds with each other despite both having a shared goal of maximizing students' achievement.

The tendency for parents and teachers to act as discrete contributors to students' learning is discouraging and thwarts the good intentions of all involved. If teachers and parents truly work together, perhaps our students would attain outcomes higher than we could have imagined. When we hear "parent involvement" or "parent engagement" in schools, the term often has multiple and varied meanings. At times, it refers to in-home activities (such as homework), and at other times it refers to parents' participation in school settings. In all actuality, it means both.

Dear future teacher,

When I started teaching, I didn't know a lot about parental involvement in schools. Early in my career (but definitely not in the first few years), I heard that students' outcomes would be greater if parents were involved in their students' education so I built some of my early teaching practices on that idea. I held parent information sessions, wrote newsletters, offered at-school family engagement activities, made phone calls, and had an open-door policy so parents and caregivers could visit our classroom when they had time to do so. One year when I was teaching kindergarten, I had a boy named Brett in my class. Brett was a high achiever academically, but had some challenges socially. He was quick to answer questions but was hard on himself if he was uncertain or answered incorrectly. One day, his mother surprised us by visiting *our classroom unannounced. I was glad to see her because I thought that having parents visit our classroom would promote students' outcomes, but our experience that day was far less than positive. Here's what happened: My students were gathered on the floor near the front of the room for a short lesson about calendar concepts. Brett's mom was sitting on a chair to the side of the room. I asked the class, "What day will it be in two days from to-day?" Brett raised his hand so I called on him, but he provided an incorrect answer. Before I could reply with support and encourage-ment for Brett to rethink his answer, his mother shouted, "Brett, that's wrong! You know the right answer. Say it! Say it! SAY IT!!" Brett cringed and literally began to shake while looking directly into my eyes. It was a horrible moment for Brett and for me. It was also a horrible moment for Brett's classmates. I impulsively held up the palm of my hand as a gesture to stop as I looked at Brett's mom and said, "Wait. Please wait." She continued over my words by shouting and repeating over and over again, "Brett, what is the answer? What is it? What is it?" She persisted until I said, "Let's all answer this one together," and my students chorally said the answer along with me. After that experience, I gained a new un-derstanding of some of the challenges Brett was facing at home, and I became contemplative about how to maintain my open-door policy despite this challenging moment.*

I wonder what you would have done.

K.

I know there are times when teachers may view parent involvement as a daunt-ing undertaking. In some cases, trust between teachers and the general public has been broken, and while there have been some places where it has been restored, the truth is that it can take a very long time to rebuild trust. Historically, this context seems to have some pretty deep roots in *A Nation at Risk*, a report by the United States National Commission on Excellence in Education, which was published in 1983 and described teachers as underprepared and underqualified. It implied that teachers were largely responsible for the lower student outcomes documented in the report. The report led to widespread concern about the quality of schools that, in many ways, still persists today. Student achievement is a result of much more than schooling—it goes all the way back to prenatal care and students' environ-mental factors at home. Our federal initiatives, including ESSA, reference parent engagement often and point out language shifts that I think are moving us in the right direction. These include the evolution of referring to "parents" as "caregivers" and "families" and reconsidering "involvement" as "engagement." Along with these language shifts comes the additional responsibility teachers have to be active collaborators with families and caregivers to promote students' outcomes. It's important to acknowledge that trust issues won't magically disappear. In fact, nearly 40 years after *A Nation at Risk* was published, trust issues remain. Yet we must find ways to bring teachers, parents, and caregivers together to become a community of support where students can learn and thrive.

We need to find ways to build bridges—not barriers—for family engagement. You may be entering our profession thinking about teaching and your students. You may be trying to make sense of the content you will teach, how you will teach it, and how your students may respond. Building bridges with parents, families, and caregivers is really about communication, and it's important that teachers provide it to families regularly. While your communication can offer information, it can also portray a tone, an attitude and feelings. Your communication might convey messages such as "I care about the progress of your student and I welcome you to join me along in a journey to educate your student this year." This type of a message can build a bridge for families to join you in promoting students' learning.

Dear future teacher,

One spring soon after I began my teaching career, my principal approached me and asked if I would be willing to implement an inclusion model in my classroom. I said yes and then I quietly thought, "wait, what does that really mean?" I wasn't sure. Even though I read about inclusion, I truly had no idea what it really was. One late August day, I received a phone call from one of my soon-to-be student's moms. She began, "I know that my son, Jared, will be in your class, and I think that you know that he has autism so I thought it would be good for both of you to meet each other before the first day of school. Can we meet soon?" I willingly accepted and planned to meet the following week. When I met Jared and his mom, it didn't take long for me to realize that I knew nothing at all about autism. Jared was unable to speak, paced a lot, and moved his hands and arms in ways that were comfortable to him and new to me. I had no training in special education and no idea what autism was or how to best teach him. I felt afraid to tell Jared's mom that I knew nothing about special education, autism, or the best approaches to teach her son. I didn't want her to think that I was unable to teach him. I listened closely and absorbed all of what she said as she explained how he communicates best, how he likes and needs consistency, and how he loves to laugh. Her approach with me was nonthreatening as she taught me how to teach her son. With true grace, Jared's mom built a bridge for us to communicate. She was open, kind, and caring as she talked with me about her son, including his needs and what works best for him. She asked if I would be comfortable using a daily journal to let her know about Jared's day, and she encouraged me to use it to ask questions if needed. She said she'd use it to let me know about his evenings and weekends as well. It was an afternoon that I have never forgotten because while it was wonderful to have a few hours to get to know a new student, it was the genuinely sensitive and caring approach that his mom used to tell me how her son learns best that made all the difference. And in hindsight, I think it would have been nearly impossible to have taught him without her.

With care,

K.

How approachable are you? Are you perceived as being open and willing to talk or closed off and shut down? Building bridges with parents, families, and caregivers takes fortitude in communication. Our school-to-home communication can be face-to-face, handwritten, or electronic. Whichever it is, the key is to establish a common ground so families know that you care and have a shared goal of helping students reach their fullest potential every day.

Families, parents, and caregivers are not a homogeneous group (Larocque et al., 2011). They are diverse in so many ways. Some will speak different languages than you, some will have different beliefs than you, and some will have different goals for their children. It's most important that you work hard to find ways to connect with each of them often. It's important to invite them to share information about their students with you. I am so encouraged when teachers request parents write them a letter at the beginning of the year to describe their students and how they learn best. How wonderful it would be if that same teacher responded and requested additional letters from parents at various times throughout the year to continue the conversation. What a marvelous request it would be!

Family and caregiver engagement comes in many different forms, and we need to be open to all of them. Have you read the book *Beyond the Bake Sale: The Essential Guide to Family–School Partnerships*? (Henderson et al., 2007)? If you haven't, I encourage you to do so soon. As the title suggests, the book advocates for the need of strong and collaborative school-to-family relationships so students can thrive. It suggests that true community and family involvement is the key to maximizing all students' achievement, and it provides wonderful ideas and suggestions that will help you develop meaningful ways to make that happen.

Greetings,

Nadira's mom wore a sari when she visited our classroom. Tamara's grandma used a walker, and Bao's dad spoke Chinese. Corinne's mom wore a lapel microphone so her daughter could hear her, and Briggette's mom held the hands of twins while carrying another soon on its way. And there was Sandy's dad, who walked in last, all alone. Parents, caregivers, and families are all different, just as a few I briefly mention here. In what ways will you be prepared to include, involve, and engage families to promote your students' success?

Each deserves your best.

K.

There's lots of agreement that parental involvement in students' education has a positive effect on their academic achievement. Indeed, our field is full of research that suggests this is true. But, as I mentioned previously, parents are not a homogeneous group so school-related activities that may work well for some will not work well not for all. Teachers need to offer a variety of opportunities for parent participation, involvement, and engagement in students' educational experiences. Research shows that what matters most is actually what parents and caregivers do at home that can promote students' success at school. We need to realize that, in many ways, parents rely on teachers for sharing information that can facilitate home involvement. Parents and caregivers need information from teachers so they can talk with their students in informed ways. When parents ask students "What did you do in school today?" students often say "Nothing," but we know that's not true. As teachers, we can do a lot to facilitate the home–school connection by writing curriculum newsletters and posting and updating students' grades in online, parent-accessible gradebooks or providing the same information for families who may have no internet access.

The key is for teachers to personalize the information when they can because that makes all the difference. Let me explain this more. It's a pretty common practice in the United States for teachers to send newsletters, memos, and notes home. The National Center for Education Statistics (NCES) reported that during the 2015–2016 school year, 89% of parents of students in kindergarten through 12th grade received general notes from school. However, only 62% of parents reported receiving notes specifically about their child (McQuiggan & Megra, 2017). That's the more concerning piece of data to know and work toward changing because we know that students learn best when they perceive that teachers care about them personally. Personal notes home with specific achievements noted and goals outlined can help students to feel connected to their learning and help parents to feel connected to their students' schooling. I know that note writing takes time, and teachers don't have a lot of it, but even a short note about an individual student's success can make all the difference.

Some barriers may at times get in the way of involving and engaging parents and caregivers in students' education. I refer to them as distancing and distraction. Distancing happens when teachers use language that can separate them from parents. At times, this can be heard in teachers' pronoun choices such as "I" and "you" used more often than "we" and "us." For example, one teacher may say to a parent, "I'd like to talk with you about what you can do to help your student improve." Another teacher may request, "I'd like to ask if we could share ideas with each other about how we can help Rylan improve?" The second example is a different way to approach a conversation about student improvement, isn't it? The first example seems to establish the teacher as the one with the knowledge about the student, while the second teacher requests a collaborative conversation. Indeed, this is something worth further contemplation. Every day, teachers make choices about which approach to use. One approach may create distance between the teacher and the parent, while the other approach can help to pull them together. Distancing also happens when we use special words and expressions that are part of our educational jargon, instead of using words and phrasing that can help families understand their students' experiences at school. It's actually a little daunting to think about all of the specialized language—jargon, acronyms, and abbreviations—teachers use with colleagues every day. When teachers include terms such as IEP, RtI, differentiation, chunking, benchmark, and leveling while speaking with each other, they have a shared understanding of their meanings. However, if jargon is used with families who do not know what the terms mean, it can create many misunderstandings that can undermine intentions of coming together to help students learn. While there are many teachers who may suggest that jargon can be a good thing because it helps us to explain things more specifically, it can—and will—distance those outside of education if we use it without explanation.

We also notice distancing with the gradual dimming of parent participation as students progress into adolescence. Parents often perceive children as needing less involvement from them as they get older, but students need continual, steady support throughout their primary and adolescence education. Adolescence can be a tough time for students socially, and teachers and families can work together to discuss students' maturational development, what to expect, and how to mutually support the changes students experience.

Distraction is another barrier to parent engagement in schools. Teachers and parents may have great intentions of coming together to collaboratively educate students, but there are other events in their lives that distract or prevent them from doing so. Perhaps a teacher wants to write a note to a parent but needs to attend to an urgent matter in the classroom, leaving them no time to write. Perhaps a teacher has meetings that consume all of their planning time so they are unable to organize a parent assembly. Perhaps parents want to attend a school event, but a late day at work gets in the way. Or perhaps a parent wants to help a student study for a test, but a younger, sick child needs attention and that prevents them from doing so. Distractions are an inevitable part of teachers' and parents' daily lives; the important part is to stay committed to a goal of working together to help students succeed.

Dear future teacher,

While some parents and caregivers will be willing to talk about schooling, some have had negative school experiences of their own that, subconsciously or not, contribute to them feeling uncomfortable in school settings. As such, they may resist interacting with teachers and school administrators. One time I had a student's parent say to me, "I know that it's important to be here [visiting my child's school] but you have to understand something: I hated school when I was a kid so I really don't like coming here." I was moved by this parent's commitment to try to set aside their own negative school experiences to be there for their student. Knowing this information can help as you begin to understand that not all parents' perceptions of schooling will be the same. Yet, as a future teacher, you will be able to help create schooling experiences that are positive for all families.

What can you do to help families participate in their students' schooling?

K.

Parent involvement and engagement should start with you as the teacher. Can you build bridges and banish barriers? If you are able to truly connect school and home, you can greet your students' families and say, "Come join me. Let's work together. The students will be better because of it. We all will."

The touchstone for teaching related to parent involvement is this: **You will improve students' achievement by engaging their families in their learning**. Research suggests that family support is essential to promoting students' learning and that students who have families who are involved in their learning achieve higher outcomes. This touchstone about parent engagement offers some implications that provide additional insight into what to do and what not to do when teaching.

TOUCHSTONE FOR TEACHING: FAMILY ENGAGEMENT WILL IMPROVE STUDENTS' LEARNING OUTCOMES

What to Do	What Not to Do
Use inclusive language such as "families" and "caregivers." It will portray respect toward and acknowledge ways they are diverse.	Don't use language that assumes students have a mom and a dad. Students are raised by many different adults.
Know who your students live with. It will help you to understand students' learning contexts.	Don't assume your students grew up as you did. Students' experiences are unique.
Ask parents and caregivers questions to gain insight into how students learn best.	Don't let distractions get in the way of communicating with parents and caregivers. It's important to prioritize connections with them.
Plan and implement varied ways for parents and caregivers to participate in students' learning.	Don't assume that one approach to including parents and caregivers in students' learning will work; one approach is too narrow to work for all.
Acknowledge parents and caregivers as individually unique and equally worthwhile.	Don't treat parents as a homogeneous group. Just like students, they are all different.

Questions for Discussion and Reflection

- What recollections do you have about your own parents' or caregivers' involvement in your education? How would you describe it?
- What is the difference between parent involvement and parent engagement? How would the outcomes be different for each?
- One of the scenarios in this chapter mentioned some of the struggles associated with Brett's mom visiting her son's classroom. What communication could Brett's teacher have with Brett's mom to begin establishing a sense of trust and care? Do you think doing so might contribute to her having a more positive attitude about Brett's learning and school? Why/why not?

CHAPTER 3

COLLABORATIVE COLLEAGUES

S chools are exciting places. Teachers, support staff, administrators, families, and community members come together to help students learn, and their collaboration can be very powerful. As a teacher, you too will participate in discussions with colleagues to find ways to help students learn. The relationships that you build will become the foundation for collaborating. One of the biggest obstacles teachers face with collaboration is not having enough time to do so. When the school day begins, teachers leave their shared spaces and enter individual classrooms, so time to collaborate can be very scarce. However, I have found that teachers are masterful at making every second count. They can skillfully grab 5 minutes in the main office, 2 minutes in the hallway, and 30 seconds at the copy machine to connect with others.

All teachers feel overwhelmed at times, and it will be natural for you to occasionally feel that way too. Perhaps you will come to feel worried about a student or uneasy about upcoming curriculum changes. During times like this, other teachers can be invaluable supports for each other. Asking for help is not always easy though, and this can be especially true for new teachers. Since it is common for new teachers to want to appear competent, at times they have been known to delay or discount a need for help. As a prospective teacher, you will benefit most from developing an ease when talking with other teachers, administrators, and support staff because they can provide you with the support you need to succeed.

Developing supportive relationships with other teachers can foster a sense of belonging in a school community. How open are you to sharing your ideas about teaching? Some teachers are unbothered by publicly sharing their teaching, while others find comfort in quietly closing classroom doors. Even if you work on your own in your classroom, other colleagues can contribute to your decision-making and problem-solving. I hope that you will be courageous when talking about what goes well with your teaching and, perhaps most important, what does not. Teachers can learn a lot from each other, and you will be able to gain insight and clarity into the nuances of teaching by talking with others.

Greetings future teacher,

It's common for teachers to describe school secretaries as those who hold everything together, and mine was no exception. Katrina was welcoming, knowledgeable, kindhearted, and polite. She was especially good at predicting new teachers' needs and was quick to provide compassion and support. Not long after I started teaching, Katrina slipped me the following note: "Please join us on the Bingo Bus. Corner of Prospect and Main. Friday at 5." I hadn't heard of this before, and I had no idea what to expect; I was intrigued by the invitation. So I met her and a group of teachers and boarded the Bingo Bus. While onboard, we talked about students, teaching, and our personal lives. Over time, I grew comfortable asking questions and listening to advice. Yes, we played Bingo too, but that was not what was important. It was the coming together, the mingling of ideas, the growing sense of trust, and the supportive, positive climate. The Bingo Bus became an important part of the first few years of my career because it gave me time to connect with other teachers (and Katrina), which nurtured my sense of belonging with my colleagues and, subsequently, my school. A Bingo Bus may not be part of the culture that you and your future colleagues will have, but I encourage you to find sustained time to spend with other teachers, both personally and professionally. I believe that is essential for you to become successful and remain in your teaching community.

K.

Getting to know other teachers personally can contribute to developing a supportive working environment, but that is not the same as collaborating with them. True collaboration involves a different skill set than having lunch together (or being on the Bingo Bus). It includes working with others to complete tasks to reach shared goals. It requires strong interpersonal skills—being open to working with others who may be similar and dissimilar to you, actively listening to what colleagues say and being respectful to their ideas as well. Collaboration also requires intrapersonal skills—the ability to know yourself, including what may help and limit you during conversations, an ability to self-reflect and self-monitor to adjust responses to others' actions so you can respond in considerate and productive ways.

Collaborators bring different strengths to their groups. Identifying tasks that are best suited for everyone can help expedite inquiry and task completion. Just like students, teachers are all smart in their own way. We all have something important that we can learn from each other.

Hi future teacher,

Have you heard the phrase "The power of two"? Doesn't it have an amazing sound to it? I just have to say it again, "The power of two." It's an immediate pronoun shifter. It changes "I" to "we" and "me" to "us" all in a matter of a second. Years ago, some of my special education colleagues introduced me to this idea, and I have never looked back. I learned about the power of two as I learned to co-teach in inclusive classrooms. The concept of teaching students with and without disabilities together has always been appealing to me. I think that's because I feel most content when everyone's together, and it's terribly troubling to me when some are left out. My experiences teaching in inclusive classrooms span well over a decade. I regularly worked side by side with special educators to teach all students together throughout the day. I once heard a teacher say, "Special educators are the pioneers of teacher collaboration." What do you think was meant by that? Special educators regularly work with classroom teachers, teacher assistants, other support staff, families, and the students themselves to share ideas as they work toward meeting shared goals to improve student learning. Maybe it will surprise you to know that some of my general educator and special educator colleagues who co-teach regularly refer to their collaborative pairings as "marriages." Even though it is in jest, I think their message has a lot of truth to it: for better or worse, they are there for each other. Some of my greatest challenges in teaching have been trying to figure out how to effectively educate in the same classroom students with and without disabilities. I got through those challenges by knowing that I didn't have to do it alone.

Don't you just love the power of two?

K.

When working in a collaborative group, a team spirit helps. While there are times to value individual productivity, true collaboration places importance on everyone pulling together to reach common goals. In schools, collaborative activities range from teacher guided inquiries to administrative-led professional development. Teachers often report that what works best for them are initiatives led by them, and research on collaboration supports this idea. Teachers can feel valued and empowered by their own actions when they are able to plan, carry out, and evaluate their own collaborative inquiries. Although administrators can be powerful at facilitating change, teachers also need to be recognized as powerful leaders in solving problems and making decisions for students and their schools. I don't mean to say that administrators need to step aside, but I want to emphasize that teachers should be leaders in collaborative efforts as well, and collaboration that includes both groups can be most productive.

Teacher collaboration is not a one-size-fits-all kind of thing. It comes in many different shapes and sizes, and for good reason. For collaboration to be most useful, it has to have a tailored fit for the teachers and schools in which it exists. That's because collaboration's strength resides in its applicability to those it serves. If it's not immediately useful to teachers, chances are high that it will not make a difference. Regardless of experience, research on teacher collaboration suggests that teachers find value in many different forms of teamwork, including paired mentoring, grade-level teaming, and professional communities of learning.

Dear future teacher,

In a perfect world, all collaborative efforts would be just-right fits for each of us. But that is not how things always go. Sometimes you will be nudged into participating when you'd rather go your own way. Many times, you will be needed in collaborative initiatives, but there will be times that the option will be entirely yours. I am hopeful that when the choice is yours, you will find endeavors that enhance your teaching and improve students' learning.

K.

As a future teacher, you will play a very important role in collaborating with other colleagues. What approach will you take? When it comes to collaboration, some teachers are go-getters. They are eager to sign up and work zealously toward goals. Other teachers are cheerleaders. They root for the effort and applaud the goals. There are also the go-alongers. They may not be so sure of the reward, but if it's good for the team, they will participate. Quite honestly, some teachers may be grumblers. They question the effort and are unconvinced of its value. What's interesting about doubt is that it can creep in to those who are also known to be the most optimistic. Understanding why colleagues may be discouraged about collaboration may help to identify solutions and bring them onboard with the work. Your approach to collaboration will matter because you can set a positive example for others, a can-do attitude, which will contribute positively to your students and strengthen your school.

Collaboration is as much about the process as it is about the product. Are you someone who revels in the process or does it ruffle your feathers? Maybe you're not sure yet. Sometimes, understanding students' learning can seem like an incomplete puzzle; no matter what you do, you just can't figure it out. In those moments, it's important to remember that none of us is as smart as all of us and sometimes we need to work with others to find solutions that we couldn't have discovered alone. We all approach solving puzzles in our own way. What is your approach? Do you put the edge pieces together first? Maybe you start with the corners. Or do you focus on the same color, shape, or size? Sometimes teacher collaboration is a lot like that. It can take many different teachers using many different approaches to find solutions to their inquiry. Trust me—there can be lots of nudging, bumping, pushing, and prodding around the table as teachers try to figure things out. Teachers often say it was worth the effort because it made them better teachers for their students and their community.

Research on teacher collaboration suggests that some types are more productive than others at improving student achievement. This one finding alone is essential to our understanding of collaboration because we need to know what it is that teachers do (and can do) to improve student learning. Research suggests that student outcomes are improved when teachers review, discuss, and respond to student data together. Additionally, research suggests that student outcomes are improved when teachers discuss curriculum and make decisions about teaching strategies together (Ronfeldt et al., 2015).

Hi future teacher,

This reminds me of a story I want to tell you. Years ago, I wanted to learn more about teacher collaboration so I began talking with some of my colleagues about it. Someone said to me, "If you really want to observe teachers who work wonders, go see Kendra and Dani." So I did. For about a month, I observed them teach together and documented their classroom interactions. One day we met together to review my notes. I attempted to describe why I thought they were effective at collaborating in the classroom. At one point, Dani interrupted me and said, "If you want to know what helps most with our collaboration, why are you observing our teaching?" I wasn't sure how to respond. As I continued to listen, she explained, "you're looking in the wrong place. If you want to know about collaboration, you have to observe our planning." Wow, that was a light bulb moment for me. Just when I thought my observations were ending, they really hadn't even begun. So I observed Kendra and Dani during their planning time. They talked about students' challenges and successes, their interests, families, and back- grounds. They talked about students' friendships and after-school activities. They were masterful at building instruction based on their shared knowledge and understanding of their students. Kendra and Dani's teamwork led to better outcomes for everyone.

What do you think about teamwork?

K.

The touchstone to take away from this chapter is **that your collaboration with colleagues will improve student achievement** and has implications about what to do and what not to do as a future teacher.

TOUCHSTONE FOR TEACHING: YOUR COLLABORATION WITH COLLEAGUES WILL IMPROVE STUDENT ACHIEVEMENT

What to Do	What Not to Do
Be courageous and ask for help. Other teachers can be your greatest support.	Don't pretend that you don't need help. Resisting assistance can negatively impact everyone.
Make it a priority to get to know others in your school community. It will help you develop a sense of belonging.	Try not to isolate yourself. Isolation can make you feel lonely and unsupported.

What to Do	What Not to Do
Find time to talk about teaching with other teachers. Social connections can help you not to feel alone.	Don't assume that all forms of teacher collaboration are the same. There are many different forms that serve different purposes.
Participate in collegial conversations about students' learning. Multiple perspectives can help you understand students' development.	Don't hesitate to talk about your different ways of seeing a problem. Be sure to communicate clearly.

Questions for Discussion and Reflection

- What strengths do you have that could contribute to being a successful collaborator?
- Think back to a time when you felt that you were part of a community. What key descriptors would you use to relate your experience? What contributed to you feeling that way?
- Why is teacher collaboration important? In what ways does it contribute to student success?
- What do you know about interpersonal and intrapersonal skills? What interpersonal and intrapersonal skills do you have? What strengths could you offer if you were to collaborate with other teachers?

PART 2

Who We Teach

CHAPTER 4

TEACHING WITH RELEVANCE

Dear future teacher,

Before thinking about what you will teach, think about who you will teach. Start there, with your students.

K.

All students are diverse. They have different backgrounds, experiences, and perspectives that they bring into classrooms every day. They differ with race, class, gender, ethnicity, ability, language, religion, sexual orientation, family construct, and on and on. Once I had the opportunity to observe a student teacher talk with third graders about differences. I was looking forward to hearing ways that she would facilitate a conversation about diversity. During a very important moment of instruction, the student teacher said, "We are all different, but we are really all the same" and then she went on to discuss ways that her students were alike. After the lesson, we talked about her teaching, and at one point I said, "I think that you missed a really important opportunity to talk about ways your students are different. Do you remember instances in your lesson that you could have done so?" She was not sure. So we recalled the lesson together and reflected on moments when she could have talked with her students about ways they were different from each other. She said, "To be honest, I haven't put a lot of thought into how to teach about diversity before this conversation." This student teacher's approach to talking about diversity is actually quite common among aspiring teachers. I've heard prospective teachers say they aren't sure about how to talk about "that topic" because it seems taboo or it might be off limits in discussions. What do you think about that? While I agree that it's important for students to recognize their commonalities, perhaps it's even more important for them to acknowledge and talk about individual differences. I say this because it can help students to know that not everyone is the same, to begin to understand that other people have different perspectives, ideas, and opinions unlike their own. This can lead to learning to respect and value diversity.

Individual differences make us uniquely ourselves and contribute to our individual strengths. Your future students will need time to talk about ways they are different from each other, to learn about and understand differences in others so they can appreciate and accept themselves and their classmates.

Dear future teacher,

I wish that we lived in a world where everybody was comfortable talking about everything. If that were true, I would welcome everyone into a great big conversation about diversity. I don't mean a conversation where we would talk about what diversity is because we already do a lot of that. I mean an open, authentic conversation so I could genuinely learn what it's like to be you, so you could completely learn what it's like to be me, and everyone could fully learn what it's like to be each other. I think that would be one of the most important conversations we could ever have, don't you?

Daydreaming,

K.

As a whole, teacher and student demographics differ considerably. Nearly 80% of the teachers in the United States are White, middle-class females. In contrast, about 51% of our students identify as non-White and approximately 58% of them currently live in poverty (McFarland, Hussar, Zhang, et.al, 2019). These statistics imply that teachers' and students' cultures are likely to be very different from each other. Learning for Justice, an organization that provides resources for educators to teach students to respect and appreciate differences, refers to what I am talking about as a "cultural gap between students and teachers" (2022). They explain that it's especially important for teachers to develop an understanding of their students' cultures so that they can develop a supportive responsiveness to them. Gloria Ladson-Billings developed the notion of culturally relevant teaching as a pedagogy that is "specifically committed to collective, not merely individual empowerment" (Ladson-Billings, 1995, p. 160). She argues for its importance in promoting "the academic success of African American and other children who have not been well served by our nation's public schools" (p. 159). As a future educator, what will you do to work toward creating a classroom that can promote individual and collective empowerment, for each student and for all cultures—especially for those who have been regularly marginalized in our society? What will you do to ensure that all students feel and are meaningfully connected you and your classroom, to what you say, what you do, and what you teach? Culturally relevant teaching requires all of us working together to perceive, portray, and teach students that every single one of us and all cultures are "equally worthwhile" (Learning for Justice, 1997).

Dear future teacher,

while it will be important for you to learn all that you can about your students' backgrounds, the goal is to know how to support-ively respond to them. Doing so will help you relate to their lives. Please remember this: if your students don't feel culturally related to you or your teaching, it is very likely that they will resist learn-ing from you. How can you ensure that doesn't happen?

Keep thinking,

K.

We all have cultural identities. How would you explain yours? A cultural identity refers to how we describe and express ourselves based on the different social groups that we are part of, such as our race, class, and gender. Our cultural identities are also described by our cognitive and physical ability, language, and religion. But I'm not finished yet—the list would also include sexual orientation, ethnicity, political party, and family construct. And many people might say that's only a start to the list! It is important for you to be able to distinguish your own cultural identity because it becomes a lot like a lens you look through as you perceive and interact with students, colleagues, schools, and communities. I once heard someone say, "All teachers have their own lens that they look through when they teach." The statement suggested that teachers' viewpoints are informed by the experiences, beliefs, and perspectives they bring to teaching. I'd like to propose that perhaps the most useful aspect of this analogy is recognizing that your "lens" can also act as a filter that enhances some things while reducing others. When we think about it that way, your lens (i.e., your cultural identity) may either help or hinder your capacity to understand and relate to students. Let me put it this way: when teachers' and students' cultures are similar, teachers have a greater likelihood of being able to understand students' lives. They may assume students' experiences at home, for example, are similar to their own, and in situations like that, teachers' assumptions about students may, at times, be quite accurate. On the other hand, when teachers have cultures that are dissimilar to those of their students, they may be uncertain about their students' experiences and this may lead to unconscious and inaccurate assumptions about their lives. If and when this happens, stereotyping, bias, and prejudice may go unnoticed, and in those situations, no one wins.

We all have biases, ways that we may think about or favor ideas or people over others. It is essential that teachers work especially hard at knowing their own biases and work toward eliminating them. In what ways do you think teachers' biases could inform their teaching? Might a teacher with a bias against certain groups of people treat students of that group differently than other students? Biases can harm everyone, especially if teachers have negative bias (unconscious or not) toward students. Teachers' bias can influence their actions about who is called on to participate more often in class, how much attention students are provided, and who might achieve more than others. How might teachers begin to identify their own biases? How might you begin to so?

Since we don't often talk about cultural identities, aspiring teachers may not always be consciously aware of the influences their beliefs and values will have on their teaching practices. They may, for example, portray a conscious or unconscious cultural bias, even subtly, during interactions with students and with the instructional materials they select. As a future teacher, it is important to be forward thinking, to contemplate and identify ways that you can implement antibias teaching into your future classroom.

I wonder, do you think that classrooms can be free from bias? In other words, do you think that teachers can create classrooms or other learning spaces that are genuinely free from prejudice, stereotyping, and unfairness toward individuals and different cultures? Many veteran teachers suggest that it's easiest to do this if we start when students are young—and I agree. Antibias teaching is not new to early childhood educators; many have been creating antibias learning environments and implementing antibias curriculum for decades. There is much to learn from books such as *Anti-Bias Education for Young Children and Ourselves* by Louise Derman-Sparks and J. O. Edwards (2010). It offers insight into how, even with very young children, we can—and should—begin important conversations about diversity. Early childhood educators are quick to say young children notice differences and want to talk about them. I've heard them explain, for example, "Kindergartners want to know why skin color is different, or why someone can't walk or talk in the same way others can." Some adults in young children's lives may feel inclined to squelch such inquiries by saying, "That's not polite. It's too personal. That's private. Don't ask that." Indeed, at a very young age, children are often told not to talk about diversity topics so when topics such as race, class, or religion are mentioned when they are older, they are uncomfortable participating in the discussions. If we start conversations when students are young, they can learn to respect, appreciate, and value differences in themselves, their classmates, and the larger community.

Dear future teacher,

One of my mentors once told me, "It's not our differences that separate us, it's our attitudes about differences that keep us apart." Gosh, that's powerful, isn't it?

I wonder what you're thinking.

K.

Regardless of grade level, research suggests that students benefit most from curriculum that includes connections to their own lives and builds on their strengths and interests. While you may find the idea of including students' backgrounds and interests in the curriculum appealing, the reality is that at the onset of your teaching, you will likely be provided with a prescribed curriculum that you are asked to follow and implement. This will provide you with an immediate challenge that, I think, can be overcome with a little creativity on your part. The goal is to personalize the curriculum, to make it relatable—to make it relevant to students' lives—everywhere it is possible to do so. Good teachers do this every day by including students' interests into lessons, by providing students with literature that includes characters and settings that are culturally relatable to them, by prioritizing time for students to talk openly about their interests, and by addressing hard topics when they arise, topics such as bias, stereotyping, and prejudice. Such a curriculum would also include implementing classroom procedures associated with fairness, ensuring all students' voices are heard and that all students feel valued as individuals and as important members of the class.

Teachers who value making their instruction relevant to their students purposely promote students from underrepresented and dominant cultures to actively participate in discussions and activities together. For example, teachers may heterogeneously group students of different races or cultures together with the intention of working toward academic and social goals. When students are grouped heterogeneously, they bring diverse perspectives that will enhance their learning. Grouping arrangements such as this portray that all students have something of value that can be useful to the group. Administrators and teachers can plan activities to support community-wide conversations on topics about cultural differences with the goal of recognizing and eliminating stereotyping and bias. Ideas such as these support the notion that we are stronger when we are together.

Dear future teacher,

I have a question for you: do you think it is equally important to talk about cultural differences as it is to talk about academic content? I wonder how you would respond. I'd like to ask you to reflect on that question while I tell you about an experience, which, to a large extent, continues to influence my teaching today. The narrative I am about to tell you is an example of something that didn't go as well as it could have. I mean, wish it had gone much better than it did. I offer it to you as something to learn from.

About 12 years into teaching and while enrolled in a doctoral program, I was asked to participate in a school–university collaborative to support students with social, emotional, and behavioral challenges. To prepare for entry, I met with the school principal and an eighth-grade teacher I was asked to co-teach with. We discussed students' academic goals and social needs and planned the lessons together. On our first day, students entered and sat down; I counted eight in the class. When it was time to begin, I started introducing early algebra concepts. Students were quiet so I continued until Yolanda abruptly stood up, slammed her hands on the desk, and screamed at me, "I don't care about math. You don't know me. Why does this matter? I've got twin babies at home, and they're sick so why should I care about math?" That was one of the hardest moments of my teaching career. I had no idea what to do; my thinking felt blocked. I sat down and said, "I'm sorry." Then, I decided to scrap the math lesson and listen instead. Yolanda's classmates took the moment as an entryway for their own sharing. They talked about their lives, not about math. At one point, I looked over at my co-teacher, and she nodded her head with an understanding, agreeing with the discussion's direction. When class period ended, students left the classroom, but Yolanda stayed behind. I thought she was going to say something, but she didn't. Instead, she looked into my eyes in a way that said, "I know you understand me better now. You're getting to know me." In subsequent classes, Yolanda talked about her children and, although reluctant at times, participated in lessons. In hindsight, I definitely didn't teach math on that first day, but perhaps something else was achieved. What do you think? What could I have done differently? Over time, Yolanda pushed me to look at schooling more broadly, and my experiences with her made me begin to ask hard questions, such as the following: Do our schools work for all students? Who don't they work for, and what are we going to do about it? When I met Yolanda, I didn't know about culturally relevant teaching practices. If I had, I am sure that I would have done so much differently. I would have started by getting to know her personally— her hopes and fears for herself and for her children. I would have thought of knowing who she is first and then worked on planning lessons with her (and the rest of her classmates) in mind. Teaching with cultural relevancy is so very important to everyone.

Please join me on this.

K.

I've often thought about students' learning contexts and contemplated what teachers can do to establish supportive and productive learning environments for students. Future teachers might initially be inclined to focus on the physical aspects of classrooms contexts, such as wall displays, furniture arrangement, and learning materials. Indeed, these are important. However, I'd like to suggest that students' learning contexts are perhaps even more powerfully shaped by teachers' language. Perhaps it is a new idea for you to think about language as a context for learning—but doesn't all learning reside in language? Teachers who value culturally relevant teaching are purposely considerate with the language they use with their students, students' families, school staff, and communities. They are also very insistent on the language choices that their students use when they talk with each other. One time, I had a professor who established ground rules during class, and one of the rules was "No put-downs of self or others." That's such a great rule, isn't it? We all know that words can be hurtful or helpful; they can be exclusive or inclusive. Culturally relevant teachers use language that is intentionally inclusive and helpful toward facilitating all students' learning. As a future teacher, it will be essential for you to give considerable thought to your language choices. I encourage you to be sensitive, thoughtful, and scrupulous about the language and word choices you use, and I suggest you teach your students to do the same. I suggest this because unintentional bias, stereotyping, and prejudice can seep into language and create unfair learning contexts for students. Culturally relevant teachers show particular care for their word choice, and I ask you to do the same.

Culturally relevant teaching holds great promise for our teachers, students, schools, and communities. The touchstone to take away from this chapter is this: **You will improve students' outcomes if your teaching is relevant to their cultures** (Ladson-Billings, 1995; Aronson & Laughter, 2016). If you were to become a culturally relevant teacher, what would you do? What wouldn't you do?

TOUCHSTONE FOR TEACHING: YOU WILL IMPROVE STUDENTS' OUTCOMES IF YOUR TEACHING IS RELEVANT TO THEIR CULTURES

What to Do	What Not to Do
Recognize your own cultural identity. Knowing the origins of your beliefs and values will help you understand yourself, including any biases you may have.	Don't think that using culturally relevant teaching practices is only about individual student cultures. It can be the starting place for helping to create a socially just society for all people of all cultures.
Take time to learn about your students' cultures. It will help you to know them personally.	Don't assume your cultural identity is fixed. Our identities change over time as we learn and understand people and ideas differently.
Provide time for students to talk about cultural differences. Talking and listening to others helps to develop an understanding of others' lives.	Don't assume that all students' cultures are the same. Each has a unique background and lived experience that has value and is worth knowing.

What to Do	What Not to Do
Teach students about the negative effects of bias, stereotypes, and prejudice. Students can learn to recognize and stop injustices when they see them.	Don't be afraid to talk about differences. Your fear will not help students to learn about others.
Use language that shows respect and support for all people and cultures. Supportive language can encourage students to learn.	Don't ignore bias, stereotyping, and prejudice if you hear it. Your silence will be perceived as approval.
Plan, teach, and implement culturally relevant lessons. If your teaching isn't relevant to your students' lives, they will resist learning from you.	Don't think that teaching with cultural relevancy is something that has a finish line. It defines and describes a never-ending process.

Questions for Discussion and Reflection

- What is meant by culturally relevant teaching? What would be some indicators of teaching that is relevant to students' lives?
- What does this quote mean to you: "It is not our differences that separate us. It's our attitudes about differences that keep us apart"? What would be an example of this?
- What are some of your own cultural biases? How do you feel about talking about your own biases? What makes you feel that way?
- How would you as a teacher learn about students' cultural backgrounds? In what ways could you include this information in a lesson?

CHAPTER 5

INCLUSIVE CLASSROOM COMMUNITIES

❝ You are welcome here. You already fit in, and you already belong. You already have me on your side. I invite you to come along with me so we can learn together." Wouldn't it be grand if every member of a school community said that to each other at the start of each day? Do you think that is possible? What would it take to make it possible?

I once heard a saying: *Ora na azu nwa*, which is a proverb from Igbo, Nigeria. It translates to our familiar saying, It takes a whole village to raise a child. What a wonderful thought! It reminds us that students need everyone in their community to work together, with each doing their own part, to support and encourage their development. Students are members of different communities around the world, and when their communities provide them with care and support, they thrive.

All schools have their own, unique communities, and while they can be very welcoming and supportive places, we need to recognize that they do not become that way automatically. While there is no specific formula for creating supportive communities, some elements have been found to keep members together.

Greetings future teacher,

All learning spaces—from preschools to graduate school classrooms—can be places where teachers intentionally create supportive learning communities for their students. Can you think back to a time when you truly felt part of a community? Perhaps it was when you were in a school club, on a sports team, in Scouts, or at a family reunion. When you think about your experiences, can you identify what it was that made you feel that way? If we had a chance to compare our responses, I imagine there would be some similarities because supportive communities evoke feelings that are often universally alike. Perhaps your community provided you with a sense of belonging, mutual liking, and trust. Perhaps you reflected on cooperating with others to reach a shared goal. All of these elements are central to creating and maintaining a classroom community, and as a future teacher, it will be important for you to work toward embedding these elements into your daily teaching. I never really thought about intentionally creating learning communities before studying Mara Sapon-Shevin's work (1999), and I've found such value in it that I encourage you to do the same. At one point, I assumed that supportive school communities were nearly always derived from happenstance, but I was not right about that. I have learned that teachers and school leaders can and should develop and implement policies, activities, and programs that can create and sustain supportive school communities for students, teachers, and families.

K.

Students are keen observers and, just like us, they can sense when they are part of a community and when they are not. They can tell when they feel a sense of belonging and when they don't. I am convinced that all students want to belong, to be liked and valued. They want and need their communities to joyfully acknowledge their strengths and compassionately support their challenges. I wonder, do you think it would be possible for you to create a classroom community such as that for your future students? I am not asking if you can do this for a few students or some students or most students; I am referring to all students, every single one of them, because I am certain that every single one of them wants and needs a supportive learning community to be fully successful in school. I ask this of you because at times, some teachers humbly admit they do not know how to include all students, especially students with disabilities, in all aspects of their classroom communities. While I greatly appreciate their honesty, I am deeply troubled by their confession. You see, students with disabilities are perhaps those most vulnerable to being socially marginalized and excluded from their peer groups and, as such, have an unyielding need for teachers to competently pave the way for their full participation. Teachers can do this by intentionally establishing and sustaining safe, caring, supportive classroom communities.

I have learned that classroom communities are developed when teachers thoughtfully plan and implement activities for students to get to know each other personally. These activities are often referred to as community builders. Teachers can pose questions for students to answer so they can share their interests, hobbies, and future goals, for example. When selecting questions for community builders, it's important to choose questions students perceive as safe to answer and to avoid questions that could embarrass students or make them feel intimidated or vulnerable. Questions that focus on family construct, living arrangements, and even friendship groups, for example, can be uncomfortable for some students to answer. Therefore, it's best to include questions that all students can feel comfortable answering.

Teachers can implement class meetings so students can talk about new events in their lives, recent achievements, or even deep concerns or worries. Class meetings provide opportunities for students and teachers to come together to offer each other care, support, and encouragement. The goal is similar for community builders and class meetings; it provides time in the school day for students and teachers to learn about each other personally, rather than a time to discuss content of daily lessons. Students need opportunities to get to know their classmates so they can come together as a community of support for each other.

Dear future teacher,

Maya was born premature and had some medical concerns that were still being resolved when she entered first grade. Her lungs were still not fully functioning so she had a tracheotomy that helped her breathe. The trach made it challenging for Maya to talk, but she learned that covering it with her finger helped a lot. Her classmates were naturally curious about Maya's trach, and they had lots of questions. Maya was comfortable—quite eagerly so— talking about it. So Maya's mom was invited to join a class meeting where Maya could talk about her trach and her mom could answer students' questions. The meeting went well as Maya and her mom explained what it was, how it worked, and why Maya needed it.

Although Maya's classmates shared ideas about their own lives during the meeting too, the focus drifted back to Maya. The meeting gave students opportunities to ask questions openly, in a safe space, about physical abilities and differences. This seemed to help them dismiss inaccurate assumptions about Maya and contributed to developing more positive attitudes toward her and (hopefully) about ability differences in general. Maya's mom's participation in the meeting was also important because it helped her to trust that the classroom community would accept and support her daughter just as she was. I believe that conversations such as this can help all of us to develop more positive and accepting attitudes about different abilities and differences overall.

Do you think so too?

I so hope you do,

K.

The idea of educating students with and without disabilities together is often referred to as inclusive education or inclusion, and it's not a new idea to our field. Research has indicated time and again that all students—those with and without disabilities—can benefit from inclusive education practices. But knowing that inclusion can benefit all students and knowing how to implement it well are two different things. One time when I was at a conference about inclusive education, one of my colleagues said, "It's easy to be bad at inclusion." A classroom teacher added, "If all you want to do is put students with and without disabilities together in the same classroom, that's easy. But if your goal is to truly maximize all students' learning when they're all together, now that's another story." Comments such as these reveal that teaching in inclusive classrooms can be a very challenging endeavor.

Dear future teacher,

While I hope that you will feel completely prepared to teach in inclusive classrooms before your first day teaching, the reality is that you probably won't. I say this because it is not possible for you to learn all there is to know about all of the different academic, physical, social, and emotional challenges that your future students will have—you haven't met them yet! Perhaps the best that you can do right now is to begin to establish a structure for their success. I mean that you can begin to learn how to prepare for your future students' arrival now, well before they enter your classroom.

It's time to start. I believe in you,

K.

There are times when all of us have felt uncomfortable when trying something new. When something is unfamiliar, it can take time to relax into it. Perhaps when you teach, it may be the first time that you interact with a student who uses a wheelchair, who has a tracheotomy, or who cannot speak or hear. It's important not to let those uneasy feelings of something new or unfamiliar become barriers to your interactions. So I ask you to proceed thoughtfully. Be open and receptive to learning how to teach students with all ability differences, and strive toward developing an ease, comfort, and skill with teaching them well.

Dear future teacher,

Sorry to write again so soon, but I really wanted to tell you about this wonderful poster I came across that's been powerfully etched in my mind ever since. The entire background was bright yellow, and there was an outline of a jar drawn in the center of it with this saying stuck onto it: "Label Jars, Not People."

I love it!

K.

Our research suggests that teachers' attitudes about teaching students with disabilities are perhaps more influential than any other in-school factor in contributing to their academic, social, and emotional success. So how would you describe your attitudes about teaching students with disabilities? Would you say that your attitudes are accepting and positive, or do you have uncertainty or feel unfavorably about doing so? As I believe you know, our classrooms are increasingly diverse places. Approximately 80% of students with disabilities spend at least half of their day in general education classrooms (McFarland, Hussar & Zhang, 2019). Therefore, at some point in your career, you will inevitably have students with disabilities in your classroom who will need you to portray positive, accepting attitudes about teaching them. They will also need you to help their classmates develop and portray positive, accepting attitudes about them.

All students want and need to experience daily respect and acceptance by their peers, but unfortunately, this is not reality for every student. Students can say very hurtful things to each other. I've observed students shout put-downs, voice derogatory comments, and make negative gestures to other students, and I bet you have too. It can be awful for students who are on the receiving end of such mocking. It can also be awful for students who observe it. As a future teacher, it will be important for you to prevent, interrupt, and respond to such statements and actions. Remember, if you do or say nothing, it will be interpreted as your approval. Our goal is for students to accept differences, which requires teachers to provide authentic opportunities for all students to interact and learn about differences and also to promote mutual respect and acceptance. In addition, teachers can work toward facilitating students' development of courage and tenacity so they can become allies for each other.

While we often think of inclusive education as an initiative that focuses on teaching students with and without disabilities together, it's important to know that inclusion now refers to more than ability differences. It's about intentionally creating learning environments where all students are safe, respected, and belong. Teachers who have an inclusive education philosophy embrace all forms of diversity and welcome all students into their classrooms—including those differing in race, class, religion, gender, ability, sexual orientation, and language—and create learning environments where all students are seen and treated as equally worthwhile. They work toward creating classrooms and implementing learning experiences that portray social justice because they believe that doing so emulates a world they wish to see and wish their students to know.

Dear future teacher,

Zohan was one of my first-grade students. He was Muslim and celebrated Ramadan, which is a time of fasting for all people in the Islam faith. Prior to Ramadan, Zohan's parents talked with me to ask if I would support them by ensuring that Zohan didn't have a snack during our morning schedule. I understandingly agreed to do so. Zohan didn't initially talk with his classmates about why he was fasting, but they were curious and asked him about it. He explained that he was not eating a morning snack because it was his way of fasting during Ramadan. Students listened carefully and responded, "We'll do it too!" You can imagine how shocked I was by their response. Surprisingly, the next day, all of Zohan's classmates skipped their morning snacks, and they did so for weeks in support of Zohan. I was inspired by their determination to stand by their friend. While I know that there are many other ways that Zohan's classmates could have shown support and solidarity toward him, their choice of giving up their snacks was something real that they could do. They seemed empowered by their choice, and I believe that Zohan felt valued by their actions. What they did represented a we're-in-this-together attitude that strengthened our classroom community. How might you work toward creating future inclusive classrooms where all students advocate for each other to develop a sense of belonging, mutual liking, and trust?

K.

I am so encouraged by the many schools I have visited that emulate inclusive beliefs and practices. At times, teachers have told me about some of their students living in poverty. They explained that their families couldn't afford rent so even large families with five and more members had to move into their cars. With approximately 13,000,000 children living in poverty in the United States today, it is increasingly likely that you will someday teach students who are from low-income families. Research shows that poverty is largely linked to students' overall well-being; it can negatively impact students' social, emotional, mental, academic, and physical development. Schools—administration, teachers, and support staff—can help to ease low-income families' burdens by suggesting resources and offering empathy and understanding.

Dear future teacher,

I occasionally teach undergraduate courses that require students to observe in local elementary school classrooms, and I regularly set aside time for students to debrief what they observed and learned while in their host classrooms. One day, two of my students said that they didn't know what to do because one of their students was homeless and living in her family's car. They expressed that they thought their fifth grader hadn't showered in weeks and hadn't completed homework assignments. As a class, we brainstormed actions they could take to help. They decided to begin by talking with their host teachers and said they would report what they learned back to our class. The next time we were together, the students reported that their host teacher had talked with the student's parents and suggested possibilities of where to get housing. One suggestion was to reach out to extended family members to ask about temporarily moving in. The family ended up doing so, which seemed to give the fifth grader some hope for future security and stability. It's important for you to know that poverty can reduce your future students' chances of being successful in your classroom and school. However, there will be a lot that you can do to support your future students who come from low-income families.

Stay open to helping.

K.

When students learn in inclusive classrooms, they have opportunities to interact with students who may be socially different from them. When students are able to learn about differences from their peers in caring, supportive environments, they learn to respect ways other people are diverse. Inclusive practices can help to shift discriminatory attitudes to more accepting viewpoints toward everyone. What might teachers do to encourage that to happen?

Dear future teacher,

I want to tell you about Mandy, one of my kindergarten students who was quiet in class but lively and interactive on the playground. One day, I was introducing graphing to students and rolled out a large, canvas walk-on grid to orient students to the format of bar graphs. I said, we use this graph to represent ways that students are different and alike. I asked students to choose between three activities that they preferred: who likes to read a book, draw, or watch a movie. Students sorted themselves into the three groups and then walked onto the rolled-out grid in sorted rows to represent how many liked each activity. Then I said we could also sort boys and girls, so students moved into two different groups and then looked at me. Everyone was where I thought they would be except Mandy. She self-grouped herself with the boys instead of the girls. One of the boys said, "Mandy, you're supposed to go over where the girls are." Mandy said, "But I'm a boy." One of the girls said, "Mandy, no you're not. Look at your long hair. You're a girl." Mandy responded, "No, I'm a boy." I was completely caught off guard by this and said, "It is fine for Mandy to line up wherever she'd like." So the students and Mandy proceeded, but I am sure that moment wasn't easy for Mandy and I felt as though my activity made her very uncomfortable. As time went on, there were other instances when Mandy said that she was a boy, and her classmates began to say it as well. I knew that I needed to discuss these situations with Mandy's parents, but, as you will discover, sometimes it takes a lot of courage to talk with parents and caregivers about topics that may be perceived as deeply personal. Mandy's expression of her gender identity was certainly one of them. During a parent conference, I told Mandy's parents exactly what I just told you. Her mom and dad looked at each other, and her dad started to cry. He explained that since he didn't have a son of his own, he treated Mandy as though she were a boy. He mentioned that Mandy had been saying that she was a boy at home too. He continued to cry. He told me that Mandy liked to swim at their neighbors' house and asked to wear trunks instead of a bathing suit, so he and his wife let her do that. He cried harder and said to his wife, "What did I do wrong?" I offered, "Honestly, I don't believe that you did anything wrong, and I don't believe that you did anything to make Mandy the way that she is. She is fine just as she is." It was a hard moment because I could actually feel Mandy's dad's struggle with this topic, and I wasn't certain how to help him through it even though I wanted desperately to do so. I continued by keeping my focus on Mandy. I said, "I will do everything I can to continue to support your daughter and to help her feel welcome, safe, and accepted in our classroom." To be honest, the conversation didn't get much easier as we proceeded, but at the end of it, I was completely embraced by Mandy's parents' appreciation of my conversation with them.

Always remember to keep communication between you and your students' parents open and honest. It will make such a difference for everyone. You'll see!

K.

As you will soon discover, all students are different, and they all have a right and a need to have their teachers fully support them to grow, develop, and learn. In this chapter, I shared stories about Maya, Zohran, and Mandy as starting places for you to begin inquiring into ways your future classrooms will be diverse places and begin considering ways that you could develop open, supportive attitudes toward all students you will someday teach.

It is important for teachers to intentionally create caring, supportive inclusive classroom communities so students are respected, appreciated, valued, and encouraged to develop to their fullest potential. I hope you will work hard to offer such spaces for your students. Everyone will benefit from you doing so.

While creating inclusive classrooms can be challenging, the rewards are well worth the effort. The touchstone to take from this chapter is this: **Students' outcomes will be enhanced in inclusive classroom communities** (Sapon-Shevin, 1999). If you wanted to create an inclusive classroom community, what would you do? What wouldn't you do?

TOUCHSTONE FOR TEACHING: STUDENTS' OUTCOMES WILL BE ENHANCED IN INCLUSIVE CLASSROOM COMMUNITIES

What to Do	What Not to Do
Take time to identify what community means to you and to your students. It can serve as the starting place for creating a community in your classroom.	Don't think that there's not enough time in the day to build classroom community. Time spent building community will always be worth it.
Remember that inclusive classrooms refer to more than teaching students with and without disabilities together. They refer to classrooms where students of all differences come together to learn.	Don't assume that students are the same. Students are all different and unique in their own special ways.
Reflect on your own attitudes about differences, and work toward having positive, accepting attitudes toward all students. Remember, your attitudes will affect your students' outcomes.	Don't assume that it's easy for students to talk about differences. It can be hard, but that does not mean you should let it stop you from doing so.
Be open and receptive to learning about differences. It will help you to portray an openness with students.	Don't overlook students at any time. Your oversight may make them feel insignificant to you.
Teach students about differences. All students will benefit from learning about ways others are similar and dissimilar to them.	Don't think it's always easy to teach in inclusive classrooms. While it can be challenging, it can also be the most rewarding work you've done.

Questions for Discussion and Reflection

- How would you define inclusive classrooms? What are some characteristics of it?

- What experiences have you had with others who are dissimilar to you? What is meant by the following quote: "It's not our differences that separate us. It's our attitudes about differences that keep us apart."

- This chapter included stories about students who were different from their classmates based on ability, religion, and gender identity. Why would these three differences be important to discuss when beginning to inquire into inclusive classrooms?

- What roles did the parents represented in this chapter take in their students' education? How would teachers who have an inclusive philosophy interact with their students' parents and caregivers? What would it look like? What would it sound like?

CHAPTER 6

ENCOURAGING RESILIENCE

Dear future teacher,

I have a wonderful colleague who teaches a course on infants and toddlers.

You may question, "A course on infants and toddlers?" Yes, it is! She teaches future childcare providers how to care for the youngest children. One day she told me the content of her lesson was going to focus on teaching as a form of healing. I listened closer. She then explained that early childhood trauma was much more common than most would believe. She said it was important for future childcare providers to know the impact trauma can have on young children so they can help them cope and heal while in their care.

Teaching as a form of healing—such a powerful idea.

K.

A few years ago, Johns Hopkins University published a study revealing that nearly half of the children in the United States experience some type of trauma in their personal lives that can negatively affect their brain development and disrupt their ability to regulate emotions (Bethell et al., 2014). This study, and many that have come after, refer to childhood trauma as adverse childhood experiences (ACEs) including "exposure to violence; emotional, physical, or sexual abuse; deprivation; neglect; family discord and divorce; parental substance abuse and mental health problems; parental death or incarceration; and social discrimination" (p. 2107). All of these personal experiences can negatively impact students' in-school success, but since most traumatic events are out-of-school incidents, teachers often assume that there's not much they can do to make a difference. Research suggests, however, that this is not true; teachers can do a lot to support students who have adverse childhood experiences. As a future teacher, it is important that you become especially good at developing a trauma-sensitive approach to teaching because in doing so, you can support and encourage your students' development of resilience and perseverance to work through and overcome the challenges they may experience. You can also provide information about services and resources that can assist students and families when they may not know where to find or receive help.

Dear future teacher,

Not long into the beginning of each school year, I planned a Meet the Teacher Night, an annual, evening event where parents and caregivers would come to the school to hear about their students' curriculum and events scheduled for the year ahead. The event provided me with an opportunity to meet my students' parents, which I saw as an important moment to begin building a partnership for educating their students together.

One day after a Meet the Teacher Night, I was casually talking with one of my first graders and said, "Philip, I am glad I had a chance to meet your parents last night. They were very nice to talk with." Philip responded, "Nice? My dad seemed nice, didn't he?" I said, "Yes, he did." Then Philip said, "I know he seems nice, but he isn't." I just kept listening as Philip added, "He is mean to me and my sister and brother. He throws my brother against the wall until he cries." I said, "I didn't know that. I am sorry that's happening. Does your mother know about it?" He said, "Yes," and then he walked away. I reported this information to my building principal. She encouraged me to reach out to Philip's mother so I called her and asked her to come into the school for a meeting. Before I met with Philip's mom, I thought about what to say and how I would say it. I knew it would be important to describe what Philip said to me and explain it just as it happened.

When we met, I said, "I wanted to meet with you to let you know that I talked with Philip after Meet the Teacher Night and told him that I met you and his dad. During the conversation, Philip told me that his father throws his brother against the wall and that his brother is getting hurt by that." Philip's mom said, "Yes, he does. He won't stop. His mother lives downstairs, and he hits her a lot too." Philip's mom started to add more details about the physical abuse Philip and his siblings were experiencing. I knew that Philip's mom was confiding in me and I didn't want to break her trust, but I needed her to know that I had to report the information she was telling me. So I said, "I am glad you feel comfortable sharing this information with me and I know you are confiding in me, but the information you are sharing with me is something that I have to report." She started to cry and said, "I know you do. One of my friends told me that you are required to report things like this, which is why I am telling you." I was surprised to hear Philip's mom say that because I thought she would feel I was breaking her trust; however, what she said made sense to me. She had no other way to get help and saw me as a means toward getting help for her family. I told her I needed to convey this information to my building principal, who would be the person to file a concern with Child Protective Services. I reported the information immediately following our meeting, and my principal contacted Child Protective Services, which started to intervene with the family right away.

At that point, the process became confidential, and I didn't receive an update. However, I knew some of what Philip and his family were dealing with, so I provided a steady, reassuring presence for Philip. I was understanding when he was withdrawn in class, and I provided options for completing assignments when I could. I understood when he was quiet around classmates, and I offered empathy when he wanted to independently complete activities. I knew it would not always be easy for Philip to be emotionally and cognitively present in class, and I believed that my understanding and flexibility helped to create a learning environment that was sensitive and supportive of his needs.

It will be important for you to become a trauma-sensitive teacher.

K

When students are faced with adverse circumstances, they have many different ways of coping, reacting, and adjusting to the events that happen in their lives. Their individual ability to adjust to adversity is referred to as resilience. All students have different aptitudes associated with resilience, and each will portray it differently. You may find that some students are able to be quite positive about the most difficult situations, while others may become overwhelmingly stuck in hardships they face. It is important to know that regardless of how strong your students' resilience is, their resilience alone will not make their problems go away. The goal is to provide families with information about resources and services that can help them and to encourage students' development of a steadfast resilience, an inner personal strength, necessary to work through difficult and traumatic situations.

Dear future teacher,

I know this is not an easy topic to think about; it can feel very uncomfortable to focus on something as disheartening as childhood trauma. But it is important that you learn about it because you may have students in your future classrooms with horrific personal experiences—students who need your care, support, and understanding. Students' experiences with trauma can be complex and all-encompassing, but you will be able to do a lot to lessen the effects of it. Trust me; you can make a world of difference.

K.

Trauma of any kind can interfere with students developing and maintaining a positive self-concept (Crosby et al., 2017; Cook, 2015). Students' self-concept represents how they perceive themselves and how they interpret others' views of themselves. Students' self-concepts are acquired from their relationships with others beginning at birth and continuing throughout their life spans. A positive self-concept is not innate or fixed; it is an acquired aspect of human development that changes over time. Research has shown that a positive self-concept plays an important role in students' success in school, and traumatic events that demean, ostracize, and physically or emotionally harm students can and will negatively affect their self-concept. Trauma-sensitive teachers may notice when students' self-concepts are low and take proactive approaches toward understanding the circumstances behind it and strengthening it. Teachers may provide students with more positive, individual attention, emphasize accomplishments and successes, encourage self-acknowledgment, and facilitate supportive friendships. While all of these ideas can help, there is no simple remedy for a negative self-concept. It takes steady, consistent support, perhaps for years, to rebuild it. Be assured that, as a teacher, your efforts can be a very important part of that process.

Dear future teacher,

Jessica began first grade soon after her parents divorced. Her mother explained that her father's leaving was very abrupt and anger-filled. Jessica told her mother that she thought it was her fault that her father moved out of the house, and although both parents offered repeated assurance that she had nothing to do with them separating, Jessica continued to believe she was the cause of the split. Jessica's classroom behaviors were troubling and concerning. She crawled under her desk and curled up in a ball nearly every day. Even with gentle encouragement, it was tough to get her to join the rest of the class. One time I asked, "Jessica, why do you want to be under the desk?" She said, "Because no one likes me." I said, "Sure they do. Come here," and I took her hand as she crawled out. I wondered what could be happening in Jessica's life to make her want to hide. I didn't know. I tried to think of something I could do to help Jessica in that moment, in the context of our classroom. I called a class meeting and Jessica and her classmates joined me in a circle. I said, "Today I think Jessica needs encouragement. I'd like to ask each of you to think of something special about Jessica and share it with our class." Hands went up immediately. Students took turns expressing ideas such as "I want to be Jessica's friend" and "I like her." I watched Jessica as she listened. I wondered, "Did she hear what they were saying? Was it making a difference?" It was hard to tell. At times I talked with her individually about ways that she was important to me and to her classmates, but she seemed sad.

I decided to go back to the circle meeting, and I asked the same request of Jessica's classmates: "I think Jessica needs encouragement. Could you please tell us one reason Jessica is special to you?" Students were glad to participate. This time, I audio-recorded our discussion, all of it, every individual response. Afterward, I said, "Jessica, I made a recording of our meeting so you can listen to it any time you'd like to hear what your classmates said to you." I gave her a copy of it to take home, along with a note to her mom explaining the recording. The next day Jessica told me that she listened to the recording at home. During class that same day, Jessica asked, "Can I listen to my recording?" I said, "Sure you can," and I found a space in the classroom where Jessica could listen to her recording. For a few weeks, Jessica asked to listen to her recording every single day, and I made sure she had time to do so. I hoped it was making a difference. It was surprising to me that she asked to hear the same recording over and over again. As time went on, Jessica stopped crawling under her desk and started to join her peers more. I was hopeful that she was starting to feel more positive about herself. While I'm certain Jessica's recording wasn't the only contributor to helping her interact with her peers, I believe it helped.

Cherishing the baby steps,

K

Although teachers can do a lot to contribute to strengthening students' self-concept, it's important to remember that they should not do this work alone. It takes a team approach—including families, school counselors, social workers, and other community resources such as mental health professionals—to provide the comprehensive supports that students need. As a future teacher, it will be essential for you to communicate your concerns about students' negative self-concepts to those who can assist and support them. It takes everyone working together to positively contribute to students seeing themselves as having value, importance, and self-worth.

The effects of childhood trauma can interfere with students' developing a positive self-concept, and those trauma effects can also impede their abilities to form positive, supportive relationships with teachers and peers (Jennings, 2019). Trauma can erode students' sense of trust in others and their experiences may result in being overly cautious, hesitant, or withdrawn when provided opportunities to interact with teachers and classmates. Students who have experienced trauma may also act aggressively, with irritation or anger, when interacting with others. Teachers need to assure students that they are safe and respected. They can promote a sense of trust by using supportive communication, encouraging language and affirmations, while avoiding put-downs, criticism, and sarcasm. As a future teacher, it will be important for you to portray understanding, patience, and consistency when building relationships with students, especially students affected by traumatic events. I say this because there can be times when even the most well-intentioned teachers may respond to students in ways that could add to the effects of traumatic stress. For example, if a student refuses to participate in small-group activities, the teacher might respond by sending the student to the principal's office. In this situation, the teacher's actions may interfere with building trust with the student. Teachers who are trained to have a trauma-sensitive approach think first about the student's situation and use that information to determine appropriate student participation options. Remember, all students are capable of trusting others. Your future students' trust in you will play a big role in their success.

Dear future teacher,

One morning, a fourth grader told her teacher that she couldn't wake her mom before leaving home for school. The teacher told her principal, who called the police to check on the student's mom. When the police arrived, they found her unresponsive and near death from a heroin overdose. What an absolutely horrific experience for her fourth grader. The student will need her teacher's individual care, consideration, empathy, and support.

If that was your student, what would you do?

K.

The National Traumatic Stress Network (NCTSN), an organization created by the U.S. Congress in 2009, offers professional training and services for children and families who experience traumatic events. The NCTSN has identified multiple effects that trauma can have on students, including ways that trauma can make it difficult to "identify, express and manage emotions." Teachers observe a wide range of students' emotions every day. Students' emotions can span from generally positive, including joy, serenity, pride, and excitement, to negative, such as hate, anger, fear, and sadness. Students who display emotional well-being display balanced emotions and can often identify their origins. Identifying emotions and their causes is an important skill for students to develop because when they are able to describe how they feel, they can then learn to mentally backtrack to pinpoint events that elicited their feelings. This self-awareness provides students with the ability to control their emotions, which contributes to developing self-regulation.

Traumatic experiences can disrupt students' abilities to monitor and manage their emotions. Some experiences can trigger such intensely negative emotions in students that they become incapable of controlling them without support. For example, some students may enter your future classroom displaying a sense of anger, sadness, or hate and, regardless of future positive experiences, may continue to portray these same emotions. When asked about their feelings, they may either not be able to identify them or not understand why they feel as they do. In addition, students who have experienced trauma may carry negative emotions from previous experiences into present and future situations. Remember, traumatic experiences can powerfully disrupt emotion control (Crosby et al., 2017). Knowing that traumatic experiences can impede students' abilities to identify and control their emotions may help you to develop a sense of compassion and understanding when interacting with them. Perhaps, for example, instead of asking, "What's wrong with you?" you could ask, "How can I help?" Remember, supporting students who have traumatic experiences is not easy and it will be essential for you to seek additional supports to facilitate your students' coping and healing process.

Dear future teacher,

There's almost something magical that happens when a teacher brings out a puppet. Puppets have their own enchanting way of attracting young students' attention to nearly any topic or activity. What gives puppets their power? Students often perceive puppets as safe and nonthreatening. They also often perceive puppets' abilities to conjure up a new world, offering immediate respite from the realities of the day. For these reasons I welcomed puppets as regular visitors into my classroom each year. I used puppets to teach each lesson about different content areas and to talk with students about feelings and emotions. On occasion, I'd bring out a big, fluffy dog puppet named Floppy. Students loved him because he was enormous, and his long fuzzy fur made him look goofy and clumsy. Floppy had one particularly strong trait that he brought to our classroom: he was a trustworthy listener. When Floppy came out, all students would clamber around to tell their news. Floppy heard all kinds of stories about playground disagreements, family celebrations, and in-class activities. He heard about birthday parties, ball game competitions, pets dying, and parents divorcing. One day when Floppy came to visit, students circled him quickly. They eagerly told stories, and when it was Ashton's turn to share, he stood up, looked right at Floppy and said, "I hate you, Floppy! I hate you!" Everyone was quiet while Ashton continued with an aggressive anger, "You are so mean and I hate you!" He then ran to the back of the room and cried. What could have caused Ashton to say those things to Floppy? I knew something was wrong. Ashton's actions were terribly troubling to me.

After school, I talked with the school psychologist about Ashton's emotional outbursts and I called his mom to talk with her as well. I asked both of them to meet with me to discuss my concerns, and they agreed. During our meeting, Ashton's mom revealed that Ashton had been horribly abused by her ex-boyfriend, who had recently been convicted of abusing him. She knew that Ashton was having trouble coping, and through our discussion, it became apparent that Ashton's outbursts with the puppet were feelings that likely originated from his traumatic experiences. While the school psychologist and I gained some understanding of Ashton's situation, over time, it became evident that Ashton needed daily counseling that our school did not provide. The school psychologist and Ashton's mom found a treatment facility that could offer Ashton daily intervention counseling. While I was sad to see Ashton leave our class, it was encouraging to know that he would be with specialists who would help him overcome his traumatic experiences. In times like this, I find reassurance and hope in one of my favorite quotes, "Although the world is full of suffering, it is also full of the overcoming of it" (Helen Keller).

K.

In January 2019, the National Commission on Social, Emotional and Academic Development published *From a Nation at Risk to a Nation at Hope*, a report that describes the inherent connections between social and emotional learning (SEL) and cognitive development. The report calls for a national collaborative effort to pull the social, emotional, and cognitive areas of development together to teach the whole child. In addition, the report recommends explicitly and implicitly teaching students social and emotional skills because doing so can lead to increased academic success and decreased misbehavior, contributing to the long-range goal of developing respectful, productive citizens (The Aspen Institute National Commission on Social, Emotional and Academic Development, 2019).

As a future teacher, it is important to realize that students' social and emotional development is intrinsically bonded to cognition (i.e., thinking and processing). Research suggests that repeated exposure to traumatic experiences limit the brain's ability to return to its normal state and physiologically changes it to a state of anticipation and preparation for continuing trauma (Perry, 2005). In this way, traumatic experiences can interfere with students' social, emotional, and cognitive development. Traumatic stress can cloud the clarity necessary for cognitive problem-solving and responsible decision-making. For example, students who have experienced trauma might be cognitively unable to constructively weigh the risks associated with drug use and alcohol abuse. They might also be unable to determine short- and long-term consequences associated with befriending peers who are involved with illegal actions and crime. Instead of taking time to collect and process information carefully, students who have experienced trauma may make choices indiscriminately. But problem-solving and decision-making skills can be taught. Trauma-sensitive teachers can model problem-solving approaches, including step-by-step processes for deciding on actions to reach goals. Students can also be taught to reflect back on past actions to determine if they were satisfied with the decisions they made and, if not, to identify different ways to proceed in the future.

All students can experience trauma, and all teachers should include trauma-sensitive approaches in their teaching. All students need to be told and taught that they can overcome any adversity they experience. Teachers need to work with a team to find support for students and families who need it. Teachers can encourage resiliency in students by helping them develop respectful and trusting relationships with others, foster a positive self-concept, learn self-regulation and emotion control, and use proactive problem-solving and decision-making skills. The touchstone to take away from this chapter is: **Using trauma-sensitive approaches to teaching will enhance students' outcomes**.

TOUCHSTONE FOR TEACHING: USING TRAUMA-SENSITIVE APPROACHES TO TEACHING WILL ENHANCE STUDENTS' OUTCOMES

What to Do	What Not to Do
Take time to learn about trauma and its effects on student learning. It will help you respond in supportive ways.	Don't assume you already know how to support students with traumatic experiences. It is a complex process that requires knowing about family services and resources for help, as well as knowing about students' social, emotional, cognitive, and mental development.
Remember, all students can experience trauma. Every student's situation is unique.	Don't believe students either have or don't have resilience. Everyone has different aptitudes with it, and they can learn to develop an inner strength that includes resilience.

What to Do	What Not to Do
Facilitate healthy, positive peer-to-peer and teacher-to-student relationships. Positive relationships can provide support to help cope with stress.	Don't think traumatic experiences can be easily overcome. It can take years of focus and perseverance to do so.
Develop a trauma-sensitive approach to teaching. Your care, compassion, and understanding will help.	Don't believe some students aren't able to overcome adversity. All students need to be assured that they can overcome all obstacles.
Help students to develop a positive self-concept. Students need to learn to respect and value themselves.	Don't ignore signs of traumatic stress. Recognizing and responding quickly to students' needs is essential to their safety and recovery.
Work toward developing a circle of support for students who have traumatic experiences. A team approach is best.	Don't presume you can do this work alone. Students with traumatic experiences need a supportive team of professionals to help.

Questions for Discussion and Reflection

- What is the definition of childhood trauma? What are some characteristics of it?
- How might traumatic experiences affect students' learning?
- How can teachers respond to students who are experiencing or have experienced trauma in their lives? Would/should teachers' responses be the same for all situations? Please explain.
- What actions should teachers take when learning about students' traumatic experiences?

Fig. 6.1. Copyright © 2015 Depositphotos/gpoinstudio.

PART 3

Where We Teach

CHAPTER 7

COMMUNITIES, NEIGHBORHOODS, AND SCHOOLS

Have you given any thought to where you'd like to teach? If not, perhaps it would serve you well to do so. What type of school appeals most to you? How would it feel when you walked through its front doors? There are many more schooling options available today than there were in the past, and it's important that you understand them because you will soon be in search of a place to teach. You may have more options than you realize.

Dear future teacher,

I learned a lot from Mister Rogers. His children's television series guided my attention to some of life's most important lessons: cherish everyone, express compassion for those hurting, and above all else, offer fairness and kindness with everything you do. I remember Mister Rogers's everlasting appreciation of neighborhoods and neighbors, and I recall his gentle invitation, "won't you be my neighbor? won't you please? Please, won't you be my neighbor?" His request placed value on being interdependent with each other—I need you and you need me—to make our world a better place. But he didn't just value interdependence, he welcomed and encouraged it. There are many neighborhoods in our world today that are struggling with this concept. Unfortunately, schools can become entangled in neighborhood struggles too. How can we ensure that today's schools can both contribute to and benefit from flourishing neighborhoods? As a future teacher, we will need you to reach out to your neighbors, to invite them to collaboratively contribute to your future students' outcomes.

Won't you please?

K.

Did you know that nearly all neighborhood schools in New Orleans have been closed and replaced with charter schools? Charter schools are publicly funded, just like public schools. But unlike public schools, charter schools are run by private, mostly nonprofit organizations. Most of the time, charter schools provide parents with choices about where their students are educated, even if schools are located far from their own neighborhoods. Having a choice has inherent appeal because it offers multiple possibilities where there otherwise wouldn't be any. The appealing aspect of charter schools is that families have different schooling options for their students without any additional cost.

In 2005, Hurricane Katrina brought overwhelming devastation to New Orleans and nearby areas and "110 out of 126 public schools were completely destroyed" (Oblack, 2019). Teachers and students evacuated, and many never returned. However, those who did return came back the following year to a new school system, redesigned to provide parents with choices about which school they wanted their students to attend. The redesign effort was an attempt to fix New Orleans's historically low-performing schools, with post-Hurricane Katrina providing the timing to do so. A decade after Katrina, National Public Radio (NPR) published a comprehensive report on the progress of the New Orleans School District titled *The End of Neighborhood Schools* (Drummond & Kamenetz, 2014).

It revealed that many residents returned to New Orleans and worked tirelessly to restore their communities but soon realized that their students were unable to attend schools in their own neighborhoods. You see, although charter schools are designed to offer different schooling options for families, large student populations (such as those in New Orleans) are often assigned to schools via a lottery system. While families are able to list their top choices, technology makes final placements, which may result in students—perhaps even students from the same families—being assigned to different schools far from their homes. Interestingly, NPR reported that within the first 5 years of the school district's redesign, New Orleans students' standardized test scores were the "largest, fastest improvement ever produced in an urban public-school system" (Drummond & Kamenetz, 2014). However, not many of the New Orleans charter schools were identified as top-notch performers, and charter schools that were recognized as underperforming are now being shut down. More shutdowns means more families vying for limited classroom seats in high-demand charter schools. As you might imagine, multiple closures and school changes can be very disruptive to students, families, and communities.

New Orleans is not alone with some of these challenges. Other cities such as Chicago, Oakland, Los Angeles, and New York have also had to grapple with similar hardships resulting from school closures. At times, school closure has been the remedy for low and declining student enrollment and low and declining student performance. Still, the hard question lingers: should we—can we—restore struggling neighborhood schools instead of shutting them down? This question and the varied answers associated with it highlight one of the most controversial education topics of our time.

The National Education Association (NEA), the largest teacher and school personnel labor union in our country, recently published, *How Closing Schools Traumatizes Students and Communities*. The article reported on parent and teacher protests against shutting neighborhood schools down. It shed light on families feeling displaced and the underlying entanglements of school closures, race, and social class and how those topics are at times ignored and dismissed when discussing school shutdowns. The article highlighted an interview with book author Eve Ewing, who studied the effects of Chicago's South Side school closings. Ewing, who was a student, parent, teacher, and currently a teacher educator-partner in the district, insists that schools are an integral part of communities and, while acknowledging that they may be less than perfect, argues that schools are the heart of neighborhoods (Walker, 2019).

Dear future teacher,

I wonder, what does the idea of a school mean to you? Many of our communities and cultures perceive a school as more than a building. To many people, a school has symbolic meaning—it represents a hope in tomorrow, for example—and when it is taken away, it can be devastating to families and communities. I do not have an easy answer for ways to restore schools so they can stay open; I sure wish I did. But, I do believe that we should work together to restore what can be restored. I also do not have an easy answer about the entanglements of race, social class, and school shutdowns; again, I sure wish I did. What I do know is that all voices are equally important, and taking time to understand what is valued, what is wanted and needed in a community, is a very important part of a decision-making process about schools. These topics need to be openly and honestly discussed in schools and in neighborhoods. I know that conversations such as these can be difficult and can feel confronting because such topics affect all of us personally, but that is not a reason to sidestep them. I ask you to join me in imagining ways that schools could be (re)designed to support all neighborhoods and ways that neighborhoods could support all schools.

What would you imagine?

K.

In 1954, the *Brown vs. Board of Education* ruling made racial segregation illegal in public schools. Even though segregation became illegal, schooling for White students and students of color remained (and still remains) largely separate. In response to this concern, a 1970s federal law allowed magnet schools—a new idea—to be offered as public schools throughout our country. The main concept of magnet schools was (and is) to designate low-performing, racially segregated public schools as offering specialties such as the arts, math and science, or technology to students. The intention was (and still is) to attract students to schools based on the specialties they offer, giving students and families choices based on personal interests rather than the neighborhoods where they live.

Magnet schools frequently report students' academic success while also reporting increased family engagement, improved school culture, and higher enrollment totals. Recent research on school performance suggests that communities looking to turn around underperforming and low-enrolled schools may find magnet schools a better alternative than shutting them down (Ayscue & Siegel-Hawley, 2019).

While magnet schools offer communities a solution for creating equitable, diverse schools, they come with their own challenges. Students may need their own transportation, admissions processes can be lengthy (sometimes with no guarantees), curriculum may focus too narrowly on specialty areas, and students who may attend could become separated and disconnected from their home neighborhoods.

Dear future teacher,

I wonder where you will teach. Trust me; all schools have their advantages and challenges. Regardless, it is important that you know about and understand some of the complex differences among schools, neighborhoods, and communities because you will soon play an important role as one of their teachers. Have you thought about where you'd like to teach? How would you describe the school and its neighborhood?

K.

Unlike charter schools and magnet schools, private schools receive no state or federal funding to operate; they offer a tuition-based school choice for families. Although the cost can be substantial, some families may perceive private schools as more desirable because of perhaps more freedom with curriculum, religious-affiliation, or alignment with particular beliefs. At times, families have sought private schooling when they perceive their neighborhood schools as underperforming. Private schools regularly require students and families to participate in application processes that may be competitive and to provide personal transportation for school attendance. Since private schools require annual tuition, low-income families often cannot afford private schooling for their students. This situation, in turn, often creates private school populations that are less racially and economically diverse. Approximately 11% of our nation's students are enrolled in approximately 35,000 private schools today (McFarland et al., 2019).

Public schools educate approximately 50.8 million students in approximately 98,000 public schools each year (NCES, 2019). Public schools are funded by federal and state budgets with additional funding coming from local property taxes. Public schools offer free education to all students with access near their homes and in their communities. Public schools, by law, are required to offer students social services that private and charter schools do not always provide, such as free and reduced cost breakfasts and lunches, special education services, student aides and assistants, and school counselors and psychologists. While some private and charter schools outperform students on standardized tests, the majority of public-school students still score favorably, and most U.S. families continue to choose public schooling for their students' education.

Every school, whether charter, magnet, private or public, has a climate and culture that is uniquely its own, and as a future teacher, you will soon play an important role in contributing to both. A school's climate and culture has been found to be far more influential on students' outcomes than any particular type of school. A school's climate refers to how a school feels, and just like our weather, school climates can range from cold and unpleasant to warm and comfortable. Resent research suggests that a positive school climate can mitigate the negative impacts of poverty on students' school success (Berkowitz et al., 2017). This is an important finding because it lets us know that efforts toward developing a positive school climate can lead to improved student outcomes. Did you know that students living in poverty are 10 times more likely to drop out of school than students from higher income families (Cataldi et al., 2009)? Creating a positive school climate can help students to feel connected to school and stay in school to graduate.

At times, a school climate can be difficult to identify holistically because each school member— each teacher, administrator, student, and family—has their own perceptions about their school's climate, and their perspectives may not agree. A school climate refers to attitudes, feelings, and tone in the school. As you may have experienced in your past, a school can take on a feeling of its own.

Dear future teacher,

Sometimes my colleagues and I would take a day off from teaching to visit other schools. This was always such an exciting opportunity because we were able to get a glimpse into ways other teachers taught, while simultaneously experiencing different school climates. One school we visited exuded such a positive climate that we talked about it for years and tried in many ways to replicate it in our own school. I'd like to tell you about some of my observations because they left such an impression on me that, to this day, I continue to savor them.

From the outside, the school was unassuming. Just like many other 1950s buildings, the brick and mortar were both expected and traditional. However, the school felt very different the moment we approached its front door. Bright red, wide welcome mats carpeted the thresholds, and a colorful sign offered "Welcome! Please use the doorbell to call the main office to introduce yourself." After we did so, a greeter came to the door and opened it saying, "Welcome to our school. We're glad that you're here today. I'm a parent volunteer greeter." The greeter wore an easy-to-read name tag and led us to a desk with a well-used guest notebook that we were asked to sign. We commented on the large vase of fresh flowers atop the desk and a large poster hanging on front that read "Welcome!" in many different languages. Right from the moment we set foot in the school, we were immersed in a warm, hospitable atmosphere that, to this day, continues to be an entry-point characteristic that I have never found in another school. The greeter led us to the main office and introduced us to the principal, who also warmly welcomed us to the school. She pulled chairs out for each of us to sit around a table, and she described in detail the school's mission and values, including their deep commitment to being a welcoming and supportive student-centered and family-centered school. After our meeting, she led us through the hallways, adorned with bulletin boards that offered encouraging statements such as "Our Best Work," "Together We Are Better," and "Everything Is Possible." Every classroom door had its own welcome mat in front of it, and bold, student-autographed signs with greetings such as "Hello!" "Welcome!" and "Please Enter!" were posted nearby.

When we knocked on classroom doors, student greeters opened their classrooms to us, welcomed us in, and introduced us to teachers and classmates. Greeters provided classroom tours and offered us comfortable seating. Every classroom offered student greeters; all teachers and students extended similar sentiments. Teachers welcomed us in warm and open ways by taking time to explain student learning goals, activities, and interactions. We observed students politely and cooperatively participating in small group activities in quiet niches of their classrooms, which were defined by different carpeted areas, low bookshelves, occasional chairs, couches, and beanbags. Table lamps glowed with additional task lighting. Every classroom featured a variety of natural elements, such as hanging and potted plants, vases of flowers, and bubbling fish tanks. Classroom spaces were organized with student-accessible materials, including their own personal files, teaching and learning materials, and supplies. Restrooms offered a collection of personal care products on side tables covered with tablecloths, including a variety of soaps, lotions, tissues, and paper towels.

At the end of the day, the principal and teachers met with us and talked candidly about their whole-school study of school design so they could learn how to create a strong school climate for their students and families. They explained their commitment to portraying supportive interactions among each other, providing a warm, productive learning environment for students, and offering a welcoming, visitor-friendly school.

Have you ever visited a school that felt this way? Could all schools portray a school climate such as this? What do you think? What would it take to do so?

K

As a future teacher, it will be important for you to understand how your students and their families perceive the school's climate because research shows that a positive school climate can promote students' learning outcomes—and a negative school climate can discourage students from participating in and attending school and negatively impact their achievement. Students need to be in school to be successful in school. Research shows a direct relationship between a positive school climate and students' attendance. Students who feel supported and safe both physically and emotionally attend school more often than those who do not. Students who trust their teachers and believe their teachers care about them also attend school more often than those who do not. A positive school climate can convey a welcoming and supportive tone, which contributes positively to student participation and to their families' engagement with the school.

A school's culture, which also forms the foundation for teaching and learning, is somewhat different than the climate. A school culture refers to the beliefs, values, and mindsets that underlie and shape school members' interactions with each other. It describes how they relate to and associate with each other and what they value and find important. For example, some schools' cultures value strong athletic status, while others place value on top music performance and the arts. Just like school climate, a school's culture needs to radiate a positive, supportive quality. Schools need to offer open, welcoming and supportive communication between administrators, teachers, students, and families so their perspectives can be understood and valued. All schools and teachers need to portray and contribute to a positive culture for learning because it can provide a strong foundation for students' success.

As a future teacher, it is important for you to know that today's schools differ in many ways. School choice provides families with a variety of schooling options—charter, magnet, private, and public—that you may not have previously considered. Just as school choice provides families with different preference options about where students will be educated, school choice provides you with different employment options as you begin to search for a teaching position. Regardless of school type, each option will offer a unique school climate and culture that provides a foundation, the footing, for students' success. Research suggests that a positive school climate and culture contribute positively to students' learning. As a future teacher, you will have a very important role in contributing to your school's climate and culture. The touchstone from this chapter is: **A positive school climate and culture will promote students' outcomes**.

TOUCHSTONE FOR TEACHING: A POSITIVE SCHOOL CLIMATE AND CULTURE WILL PROMOTE STUDENTS' OUTCOMES

What to Do	What Not to Do
Embrace our interdependence with each other. Together we can create supportive and productive schools.	Don't overvalue independence. Be neighborly and take a team approach when educating students.
Understand the benefits of school choice for families. Also understand the different employment opportunities that school choice will provide for you as well.	Don't assume all schools are the same. There are many different schooling options available that need to be understood.
Be respectful of families' school choice. Decisions about students' schooling are largely personal, and each family's decisions should be respected.	Don't assume school choice is not a valuable opportunity. Having school choices empowers families to make decisions for their students.
Do all you can to foster a positive school climate. A warm and encouraging school atmosphere will enhance students' learning.	Don't leave it to school leaders to create a school climate. Every school member has a very important role in creating a positive and productive learning environment.
Take time to interact with others in a supportive and encouraging way. It will help to develop a positive, affirming school culture.	Don't use language or actions that could be perceived as negative or discouraging. Doing so could interrupt the development of a positive school culture.

Questions for Discussion and Reflection

- Explain the different types of schooling available for students. What are some characteristics of each?
- How might teachers work toward creating a positive school climate? What would it look like? What would it sound like?
- In what ways is a school's climate different from a school's culture? What are examples of each?
- Think back to one of the schools you attended as a student and write a short narrative to describe its climate. Did it work for you? Why or why not?

Fig. 7.1. Copyright © 2010 Depositphotos/Feverpitch.

CHAPTER 8

OUR CLASSROOMS

Dear future teacher,

In 2016, The Washington Post and other news networks reported a high-profile teacher union versus school district lawsuit over deplorable school and classroom conditions in the Detroit Public School District. The lawsuit reported schools with broken windows, bullet holes, black mold, rat and insect infestation, raw sewage, exposed wiring, trash in air ducts, and freezing temperatures (Brown, 2016). As you can imagine, situations such as these interfere with students' well-being and learning. School and classroom environments play an integral role in students' physical, social, emotional, mental, and cognitive development. Schools need to be places where students can thrive. It goes without saying that teachers alone cannot improve learning conditions such as those reported in Detroit. It will take government officials, schools boards, administration, and communities working together for years to repair and restore their school buildings and grounds. I invite you to take a moment to think back to when you were a student. How would you describe some of your classrooms? Were they ideal or did they lack in appeal? Do you think that they enhanced or limited your outcomes? Now, take a moment to imagine a truly optimal learning environment for your future students. What would it look like? What would you include? What would you design?

Pondering captivating classrooms,

K.

Since students spend hours in school every day, it's important to ask how the school and classroom is designed. While answering this question may seem unimportant to your future teaching, that is far from the truth. School and classroom design have been identified as major factors in impacting student learning. As a future teacher, it is important that you know about effective design elements for schools and classrooms because the choices you will someday make can enhance or perhaps hinder your future students' outcomes.

The physical environment plays a very large role in students' learning. Loris Malaguzzi, a psychologist who founded the Reggio Emilia approach to early childhood education, a child-centered and child-empowering approach to teaching, gifted us with the notion, "There are three teachers of children: adults, other children, and their physical environment" (Malaguzzi, 1998, p. 177). What does this mean? How might a physical environment "teach" children? And what could children learn from it? All of us learn as we gather information by seeing, hearing, touching, smelling, and tasting the world in which we live. We process the information to make sense of it, to understand it, and to learn from it. When students are immersed in their classrooms, they learn as they experience everything in them, including what is on the walls, the floors and the ceilings; the available materials and resources; the furniture and its arrangement; and, of course, others—teachers and students—who share their learning space with them. Viewing students' learning environment—their classroom—as a "third teacher" offers opportunities for teachers to proactively contribute to it by intentionally creating a setting where students can be fully supported to learn, grow, and thrive.

Schools and classrooms need to be safe and comfortable places with optimal resources to assist all students in reaching their fullest potential. One main research finding about school and classroom design points to the importance of including natural elements in learning spaces. Natural lighting can substantially increase student productivity and lead to improved outcomes and achievement. Schools and classroom design should incorporate "daylighting strategies," a design element that schools are utilizing more thoughtfully across our nation. Studies have found that incorporating natural light into classrooms can contribute up to 25% increase in students' academic performance compared to classrooms without natural lighting (Heschong Mahone Group, 1999). This finding is important because teachers may perceive large windows as potential student distracters and cover or block them with furniture, posters, blinds, or screens to try to keep students' attention in the classroom. While we know that students' attention needs to be on learning activities, there are other ways to guide students' focus toward in-class activities than covering classroom windows. Blocking windows can be counterproductive to promoting students' outcomes because it can dramatically reduce the natural light in the classroom.

Studies also report that students learn better in classrooms with natural light than in classrooms with artificial (i.e., bulb) lighting. However, artificial lighting, mainly fluorescent, is the most often used source of lighting in schools and classrooms. Schools' fluorescent lighting has been studied for decades, with research suggesting that since it includes a discontinuous light spectrum (i.e., flickering) and frequently emits a buzzing sound, it can increase students' stress and negatively impact learning, behavior, and mood (Kinnealey et al., 2012). Incandescent and halogen lighting offer less flickering than fluorescent lighting but are still not as ideal as natural daylight to promote learning. The goal is to ensure that natural lighting is optimized in your future classroom while decreasing artificial light when possible.

Research findings suggest that living plants are another natural element that should be included in school and classroom design (when possible) because they seem to have a natural relaxing effect on students. Including plants in students' learning spaces has been found to contribute to improved academic performance and mental health and can help to elicit calm behaviors. Living plants have also been found to contribute to improved concentration and focus, which may be especially helpful for students who have attentional concerns such as attention deficit disorder (ADD). Plants should be considered a standard design element in schools and classrooms as they offer a simple way to enhance learning environments.

Dear future teacher,

It is important that your future students learn to care for other living things, and teachers can facilitate students' responsibility and appreciation of our natural world by having plants in classrooms. Students can also learn about the symbiotic existence we have with plants. People and plants need each other to survive, and pointing this out to students is one step forward in encouraging them to care for our environment.

K.

I once read an article that compared a classroom's visual appearance to a bag of Skittles©—bright, bold, and colorful. Would that be a desirable classroom to you? Some would argue that a Skittles-colored classroom might be distracting and perhaps might contribute to students being overly excited, for example. While classroom wall color may seem insignificant, research in this area shows that we should pay closer attention to it because it has been found to have a rather significant influence when it comes to student learning.

Most school and classroom walls are painted with colors in industrial hues of white into gray. While shades of white and gray seem neutral, and while some may identify this color range as a good choice, research suggests that white is the least desirable of all color preferences. It has been found to cause eye strain, produce excessive glare, and cause vision fatigue. In addition, some research suggests hues of white and gray have been found to contribute to students' anxiety and tension (Mahnke, 1996). While I know you may not be able to do a lot about your future classroom's wall color, I believe you will be able to consciously select colors that you can use to enhance it. Since bulletin boards take up a substantial amount of classroom wall space, you will be able to add and change color in the classroom. Remember, the key is to intentionally create a positive environment that is conducive to your students' learning and to your teaching. General ideas about wall color relate to students' responses to it. For example, at times when you may want to bring excitement to your classroom, selecting bright reds, oranges, and yellows may help to promote students' enthusiasm for a topic; and when you want to bring a sense of tranquility to your students' environment, selecting cooler hues such as dimmed violets, blues, and greens will help to promote a calm and relaxing learning atmosphere (Mahnke, 1996). Research suggests that balance is best. Too much color or the lack of it (i.e., white) can overstimulate students and create feelings of stress and friction. Warm, neutral wall colors such as tans have been found to be most beneficial for students' learning (Gains & Curry, 2011).

As a future teacher, you may find it appropriate to incorporate different colors into smaller areas within your classroom. For example. if you find yourself teaching in a primary school setting, you may designate different portions of your classroom for different purposes. Classroom areas that are set aside for dramatic play or hands-on experiments, for example, would benefit from warmer hues of reds or yellows because these colors can prompt students' excitement and investigation. Another area of the same classroom might be defined as a quiet reading corner and adored with cooler hues of violets and blues to promote a relaxed, quieter atmosphere there (Mahnke, 1996).

Teacher–author Emily Style suggests that students need to have "windows and mirrors" in their curriculum and in their classroom (Style, 1988). Her expression suggests that students need "mirrors" to see representations of themselves (i.e., their cultures, the way they live) in their physical environment, including in their learning resources and teaching materials, because it acknowledges them for who they are and conjures up feelings of value and affirmation. When students see others who are culturally like them in posters on their classroom walls, in books in classroom libraries, and in teaching materials that are used, it communicates messages such as "If my culture is valued enough to be in pictures and in writing all around me, then those who selected those pictures and writing must value me too." Additionally, students also need to have metaphoric "windows" in their environment, to provide opportunities to view others' cultures that are different than their own. Such "windows" refer to teaching materials and resources in classroom environments that provide information about others' lives which can help to teach about ways cultures are dissimilar to their own. When students see cultures different than their own represented in their learning environment, they are introduced to differences while receiving communication that cultural differences are valued and accepted. Teachers who are aware of the "windows and doors" metaphor can intentionally create a learning environment portraying that their students' cultures and other cultures are both important. This can serve as a first step in helping students develop a cultural awareness and value a diverse cultural community.

While it's important for you to know the role the physical environment can have in students' learning, the largest contributor to effective classroom design resides with the ownership that students have with it, the adaptability to the space and the climate and culture that are found within it.

Dear future teacher,

My school was the kind that had teachers who stayed late and went into school on weekends to transform classrooms into learning wonderlands. When it was time for the rain forest unit, for example, my colleagues and I pushed up our sleeves, grinned ear-to-ear, and got to work! We brought in nonliving and living plants, hung out vines from ceilings, exhibited models of rain forest animals, including snakes, frogs, insects, bats, sloths, and birds. We crumpled yards and yards of rolled blue paper to make ceiling-to-floor waterfalls and meandering streams. We displayed posters, pictures, and books upon books of facts and information to promote students' rain forest inquiry. Gosh, it's a wonder that our students could even find their desks among the jungle! While we loved every minute of creating classroom transformations such as this, in hindsight, I ask myself, did our efforts promote students' learning? Did we perhaps overstimulate them? And, quite reluctantly, I also ask, why didn't we have the students design the classroom transformations? Why did we do it without them?

Hindsight is always 20/20.

K.

Teachers need to provide every possible opportunity for students to assume responsibility of their own learning because it empowers students when teachers do so. When possible, teachers also need to give some classroom design responsibility to students because in doing so, they will be able to relate to their learning environment personally.

Since classrooms are where students learn, students need to be offered opportunities to express what's working and what's not regarding classroom design. Teachers sometimes overlook asking students questions such as these: Is the lighting making it difficult for you see? Is the hallway noise making it difficult for you to concentrate? Is your seating comfortable to you? How could the classroom be organized to make learning easier for you? Teachers shouldn't assume they know answers to these questions. When possible, students should be surveyed to identify what classroom design elements could be changed. Teachers can use the information to create learning spaces with students' suggestions in mind. Ideas such as these can help to give students ownership of their classroom, which will help them feel connected to their learning environment and promote their learning outcomes.

I'm wondering if you've ever seen pictures of school desks from the 1800s? They were built with hardwoods on cast iron frames, specifically designed for row arrangement. The bench-style seats included a backrest with a desktop affixed behind it so that desks could be placed in front-to-back row formation. The bottom of the desk legs included holes so they could be bolted to classroom floors. While these desks offered sturdy seating, their design limited classroom arrangement. The desks were stationary, providing no opportunities for relocation. Indeed, classroom seating has changed considerably since that time. Classrooms now regularly include flexible seating, which offers multiple and varied seating choices for students. It is common, for example, to see flexible seating options such as cushioned chairs, beanbags, stools, wobble seats, exercise ball chairs, floor cushions, and traditional chairs all in one classroom. In the same way that seating is flexible, students' work surfaces can differ, including standard desks, low desks, tables, clipboards, and lapdesks. These flexible work surfaces provide opportunities for students to change their seating options, which has been shown to improve academic focus while increasing movement. Flexible classroom furniture options make it easier for teachers to rearrange learning spaces and make seating more accommodating and accessible for all students.

The purpose of flexible seating is to provide a wide range of options for students. Unlike standard row seating, flexible seating makes room rearrangements easier so tables can be clustered together for small group collaboration or separated for independent inquiry. When students see that desks and tables are clustered together, it portrays the message "since sitting together is valued, working together must be valued too." Providing opportunities for students to sit near each other helps them to have closer proximity so they can help each other and learn from each other.

While careful classroom design can contribute to creating a conducive indoor learning environment, many teachers have found that taking their students outdoors can prove to be beneficial for their learning and overall well-being. Teachers regularly report that students who have time outside are able to focus more on academics, be calmer, and develop an appreciation for nature.

Dear future teacher,

I'm wondering if you have heard about forest schools. They are environmental, outdoor education programs that hold classes nearly exclusively outdoors. In both fair and inclement weather, students learn outside of traditional classroom walls as they are immersed into the natural world. What do you think would be some advantages of being a student in an outdoor school?

K.

Developing a relationship with nature is not easy to do in traditional classrooms, but forest schools provide opportunities for students to do just that. Students are able to connect with nature—to learn about and experience plants and animals in their habitats, to discover different weather patterns, to see rock formations, the water cycle and the sky, and in doing so, to increase an appreciation of the natural world. Forest school curriculum is often guided by students' exploration and processing; outdoor play is valued and encouraged, offering students nature-based opportunities to learn without the boundaries and confinement of indoor classrooms.

The Children and Nature Network (2022), an organization that provides research and resources that promote outdoor education and play for youth, reports findings about the benefits of outdoor education. Outdoor settings have been shown to promote students' academic, social, and emotional development. There are a lot of lessons that you as a future teacher may be able to implement when taking students outside to learn. Perhaps you can take a class nature hike, encourage students to observe and document their natural surroundings, create nature journals to document their thoughts and feelings, collaborate with classmates to build outdoor shelters, plant flowers and vegetables, find math in nature, and on and on. Taking students outside can promote their overall health and well-being.

This chapter focused on the physical environment and the role it has in contributing to students' learning. The touchstone to take away from this chapter is: **A classroom environment can be designed to enhance students' learning**.

TOUCHSTONE FOR TEACHING: A CLASSROOM ENVIRONMENT CAN BE DESIGNED TO ENHANCE STUDENTS' LEARNING

What to Do	What Not to Do
Create a safe and comfortable classroom. Students learn best when they feel secure.	Don't overlook students' physical comfort in the classroom. If they are physically uncomfortable, it can distract them from learning.
Be sure to optimize natural lighting in the classroom. Only use artificial light when necessary.	Try not to cover windows. Students will learn best when their workspace is illuminated with natural light.
Try to include natural elements, such as plants, in your classroom. They will help students to feel relaxed and part of nature.	Don't create classrooms that feel sterile and institutional. Students' learning is heightened in classrooms that feel warm and inviting.

What to Do	What Not to Do
When possible, balance the use of color in your classroom. Either too much or too little color may contribute to unsettled and anxious emotions.	Don't assume you can't do anything about classroom wall color. Bulletin boards, screens, and posters can all be changed by teachers in ways that can enhance the color in a classroom.
Provide opportunities for students to have ownership in classroom design. Students will feel empowered to contribute to their own learning environment.	Don't design classroom spaces without student input. Students will feel a sense of belonging when they have an active, participatory role in creating it.
Find opportunities to provide outdoor learning experiences for students. Experiencing outdoor elements firsthand can enhance students' learning outcomes.	Don't confine students to indoor environments. They need opportunities to play, learn, and grow when they are in their natural world.

Questions for Discussion and Reflection

- Imagine an optimal learning environment for your future students. What would it look like?
- In this chapter, the author describes a classroom as a students' third teacher. What does that mean? What are some examples of this idea?
- What are natural elements, and why are they beneficial to have in a classroom?
- Classrooms need to be places that have "windows and mirrors." What is meant by this metaphor? What are examples of each?
- This chapter referenced ideas about flexible seating. What is it and how does it contribute positively to students' learning?
- What is meant by "outdoor school"? What are some benefits of taking students outside to learn? How would you feel about learning in an outdoor school?0

PART 4

How We Teach

CHAPTER 9

STRENGTHS-BASED, WHOLE CHILD APPROACHES TO TEACHING

This might sound counterintuitive, but it seems important that I say to you, *make sure your teaching doesn't get in the way of your students' learning.* This is perhaps the grandest piece of advice I or anyone may be able to offer you and other aspiring teachers. I know this suggestion may be perplexing, but please stay with me because I'd like to unpack it a bit with you.

You will soon discover that every moment of your teaching will afford you with an opportunity to make a choice about how you will teach. What an enormous responsibility it will be! I'd like to suggest, and perhaps all would agree, that each moment's choice should in some way be supportive to students. It makes good sense, then, for teachers to momentarily pause to self-check. Ask yourself, Will what I say or do support students' learning and development? While this sounds simple enough, I have found that it can be rather challenging because without introspection, teachers' language and actions may, at times, be quite unsupportive to students.

Dear future teacher,

It was common for my principal to meet regularly with teachers to talk about teaching and students' progress. During one of my meetings with her, she asked, "Do you have anything engaging planned for tomorrow morning?" I responded, "We're going to have a spelling bee. I think students will like it." She then paused and offered, "Can we talk a little about that?" Without hesitation, I replied, "Sure we can." She then said something that has become like a cognitive compass for me that continues to provide direction for instructional choices I make. "I'm curious," she inquired, "if you are going to have a spelling bee, might you already know who won't win before you even begin?" I said I hadn't thought of that, but yes, I could think of some students who probably wouldn't win. She then asked, "Well then, why are you going to do it? Why would you purposefully plan and implement an activity if you already know the students who won't win?" My principal's questions were rhetorical, yet the impact was swift. The questioning initiated deep contemplation about choices I made in the classroom, and it nudged forward an important and necessary growth in my professional judgment. I learned from my principal—and I have since become even more aware—that teachers' choices are not always innocuous and decisions about how to go about teaching need to be thoughtfully considered. I learned that if teachers' essential goal is to support all students' learning—and I believe it ought to be—then teachers need to ensure that they do not make choices that are unsupportive to students. You see, at first glance, a spelling bee would seem harmless, but in reflection, it requires students without spelling as a strength to publicly perform something they cannot do, made worse by peer scrutiny as an unwelcome guest. My principal's questioning had me take a step back and rethink my choice, based not on curriculum, but on students' abilities. My step back essentially became a stride forward in developing a professional judgment that I could not have developed alone. Perhaps her questioning may guide you too.

K..

Students feel most supported when they are recognized for their strengths—for what they do well, what they are good at doing, and what interests them. I would like to suggest that when considering how to teach, the most productive place to start would be with students' strengths, as a foundation for their learning and for your teaching. Students' strengths, unlike their weaknesses, naturally provide a solid base on which to build learning. Teachers who use students' strengths as a source for new learning, portray what is referred to as a strengths-based approach. They ground teaching in what students are able to do, utilize resources that are available to them and their families, and highlight their achievements, interests, and desires. At times, a strengths-based approach is also referred to as assets-centered because it highlights students' advantages and benefits, their qualities, skills, and abilities.

Teachers who use a strengths-based approach facilitate students' awareness and recognition of their own talents, aptitudes and capabilities, which can be both encouraging and empowering when learning something new (Brownlee et al., 2012). Teachers can ask students, "What are you good at doing? What interests do you have? What part of this assignment do you understand? What helps you to learn?" I find it discouraging that when some students are asked to describe what they are good at, they come up with a list far shorter than a list of things they find difficult. To me, that is most unfortunate because I believe it to be a learned response. I worry, and perhaps you might too, of the outcomes derived from students' attention being far too directed onto what they have done wrong, how they have responded incorrectly, and what they haven't gotten right, instead of highlighting the good in them, what they do right, and what they do best.

Dear future teacher,

While I sat elbow to elbow with families, students, teachers, and staff members, we watched snapshots of the school year roll across the screen. We relived sweet moments of newly formed friendships, delightful aha science experiments, hand-in-hand hallway walks, and a warm, spring breeze that embraced children's faces peering from school bus windows. Captured memories filled the room as song lyrics by Red Grammer resonated throughout and within: "See me beautiful. Look for the best in me. It's what I really am and all I want to be. It may take some time. It may be hard to find but see me beautiful. See me beautiful each and every day. Could you take a chance? Could you find a way to see me shining through in everything I do? And see me beautiful" (1986). Red's warm voice embraced our school year. The lyrics encourage me—both then and now—to see the best in everyone because if I do, I believe something good will come of it. His message assures me, and perhaps you too, that even when the search for something good in someone becomes arduous, if we look hard enough, we will find a best self that wants and needs to be known.

See your students beautiful,

K.

Teachers who take a strengths-based approach to teaching are very careful with language they use. They consciously redirect thinking and expressions away from the following thoughts: What didn't the student get right? What did you get wrong here? What needs to be fixed? Instead they focus on a strengths-based mindset, including: What is going well? How can we build upon that? What are you able to do? They steer away from deficit-based thinking and keep negative language out of their teaching and out of their students' learning environment. Contrary to a strengths-based approach, deficit thinking focuses on what's wrong, defective, broken, or needs to be fixed. A deficit approach gets in the way of students' learning because its focus resides in deficiencies, and when students' attention is repeatedly directed to what's gone wrong with their learning, "it's wrong" has an invasive way of spreading from assignments onto students themselves and their identities. The message becomes not that they have done something wrong, but that they are holistically wrong, a failure, broken and flawed. When external and internal messages combine, deep discouragement can set in, which can lead to students giving up entirely.

Strengths-based approaches have their origin in positive psychology, an area of study that focuses on strengths and overall well-being. It emphasizes the importance of identifying potential and the positive emotions associated with it (Seligman et al., 2009). Positive psychology guides us to focus on our positive experiences and encourages us to develop and gravitate toward supportive environments because they can contribute to our overall well-being.

Dear future teacher,

I consider it a good fortune that my school district asked all teachers not to use red ink when grading papers or responding to students' work—no red pens, no red pencils, no red markers, no red writing utensils of any kind. Right from its inception this initiative was universally accepted by all teachers because, with little to no need for contemplation, there was agreement that red slashes across students' work could solicit feelings of defeat and angst. We were open to using something different, and we were provided a variety of green and purple pens for grading all papers, class activities, and homework. Within weeks of receiving my new pens, I was grading students' math papers and came across one submission that had 8 out of 10 incorrect. Rather than writing -8 at the top of the paper, another teacher suggested that I write +2 with a plan of telling the student something such as, "I'd like to talk with you about your math paper. Let's take a look at these two correct here because you did these two just right. Can you tell me how you did these?" Truly, I initially thought that this suggestion was without merit. However, the longer I inquired into this approach, the more worthwhile the shift in perspective and action became. Encouraging students to focus on what they did correctly can help to establish a positive tone for teachers to offer strengths-based feedback and to begin future goal-setting. I offer this to you as a small, yet notable, example of a strengths-based approach and invite you to carry out similar responses to offer strengths-based feedback to your own students. I suppose that some good fortune came to me twice—with the pens and with a colleague guiding me to focus on what students did correctly. A strengths-based approach can have a positive effect on students. Do you think so too?

K.

P.S. I still don't use red ink!

While students benefit from teachers' strength-based approaches, the greater value is when students assume their own strengths-based thinking about themselves because doing so can lead to individual empowerment. Students can be empowered by identifying their own strengths and learning to intentionally use them as a foundation when learning something new. Teachers can assist students' growth in this empowerment by guiding them toward interpreting mistakes and errors as a normal part of the learning process. Just as important, teachers can guide students toward perceiving errors or mistakes as future goals to work toward meeting. In addition, students' goal-setting can foster the development of their individual accountability, which can develop a sense of responsibility for their actions, choices, and outcomes associated with identified goals.

It's important to recognize that a strengths-based approach does not mean that incorrect answers or inaccuracies are ignored. Instead, a strengths-based approach acknowledges misconceptions, but rather than solely pointing out what was incorrect, a strengths-based approach reconceptualizes students' inaccuracies by focusing on solutions and identifying goals that mutually developed with students. Again, it can be very empowering to students to set their own goals, and as a future teacher, it will be beneficial to your students if you give them regular opportunities to do so. Goals can be very motivational to students; they can provide direction for students' actions and growth. Reframing what students didn't do correctly as goals to meet in the future shifts what could be a discouraging moment to one filled with encouragement and possibility. Which approach do you think would more likely promote students' learning?

The premise of a strengths-based approach is holistic interaction and support by focusing on what is going well. Students benefit most when teachers do not limit their focus to academics but widen it to include students' social, emotional, mental, and physical development. This holistic perspective of teaching is referred to as teaching the whole child, and it coincides well with a strengths-based approach because students' benefit most when they are fully seen (whole child) and fully supported (strengths-based) for whom they fully are.

The whole child approach casts an overarching concern onto every aspect of students' development to ensure students are "healthy, safe, engaged, supported and challenged" (Griffith, 2019, p. 90). While in some ways it can be helpful to address one area of students' needs in terms of academic, social, emotional, mental, or physical, applying this type of sorting (i.e., separating) can reinforce a partitioning paradigm that the whole child approach attempts to change (Slade & Griffith, 2013). In other words, the whole child approach recognizes that all areas of students' growth develop interdependently and cannot and should not be addressed separately.

Dear future teacher,

Amy was struggling with learning to read, and despite offering her independent review lessons, she was making little to no progress. I was increasingly concerned. Amy's parents were concerned too. We met and came up with some ideas about how to help her. I contemplated what to do next and talked about my concerns with a colleague who simply asked, "Are you sure Amy can see the text?" "Oh gosh," I said, "we hadn't thought of that." Afterward, I talked with Amy's parents about possible eyesight issues and they took her to an eye doctor. Guess what they discovered? Amy needed glasses. Why hadn't we thought of Amy's eyesight development first? Why were we solely focused on Amy's academics? Remember, to teach the whole child, teachers need to view the child holistically.

K.

In some instances, the whole child approach may be applied with less effort in elementary school settings than in middle and high schools. I say this because elementary school teachers' schedules are often designed so they teach the same students throughout the entire day. This schedule typically includes more than 6 hours spent with students, and time with students is a necessity for teachers who take a whole child approach. In contrast, many middle and high school teachers have fewer than 45 minutes each day to interact with students, which can make it challenging to get to know students well. In instances such as this, teachers often say that they benefit most by using team approaches so teachers and support staff can collectively share student observations, insights, and interactions with each other to collaboratively see students holistically.

Dear future teacher,

One of my friends teaches in a school where her fifth grade students switch classes every 43 minutes, which doesn't give much time for her and her colleagues to get to know their students personally. The teachers get together each quarter to talk about each student individually, identifying if and when each teacher had a personal connection with each student. If they find that there hasn't been a personal connection made, the teachers make a concerted plan to talk with the students, to ensure the students feel and are seen and heard. They work toward learning about students holistically, understanding their social and emotional well-being (beyond academics) as they try to pinpoint areas of strength and areas that may need support. Only when teachers know what students need can they help their students' needs be met.

K.

In many ways, our nation's school system evaluates students' development nearly exclusively on standardized test scores. While these data provide some insight into students' growth, test scores actually represent a very small aspect of students' development. Starting with the No Child Left Behind Act (NCLB, 2002–2015) and continuing through the current Every Student Succeeds Act (ESSA, 2015–), our nation often reports test scores alone to identify students' and school progress. If we value a whole child approach to teaching, then we need to measure students' growth, not as stand-alone bits of data, but as holistic narratives that fully represent who students are. The whole child approach has the potential to have a larger-scaled impact, beyond students, teachers, and schools, to broaden a common perspective on what is most valued regarding students and their success (Griffin, 2019). The whole child approach can portray the necessity of knowing, understanding, and supporting all aspects of students' development—for their good and for the good of our society.

The touchstone for this chapter is: **A whole child, strengths-based approach will promote students' learning**.

TOUCHSTONE FOR TEACHING: A WHOLE CHILD, STRENGTHS-BASED APPROACH WILL PROMOTE STUDENTS' LEARNING

What to Do	What Not to Do
Ask students to identify their strengths. All students have strengths that need to be known and acknowledged.	Don't focus students' attention on what went wrong and on mistakes they made. Doing so will discourage them.
Ask students to identify their challenges, not as what's wrong but as future goals to be met.	Don't assume that you can recognize students' strengths and challenges on your own. It will help to ask students about it.
Include students when identifying their future goals. Students who are focused on goals develop an inner responsibility for achieving them.	Don't create students' goals without them. This would have the ownership of students' goals reside with you, not with them.
Develop a solutions-focused mindset. Focusing on solutions is proactive, and students will perceive it as support.	Don't use a deficits-focused mindset. It will lead to negative thinking and unproductive communication.
Take the whole child approach when teaching. Focus your attention on a holistic perspective of students' development.	Don't analyze and interpret different areas of students' development separately. It will lead to a shallow and insufficient perspective of their growth.
Implement whole child and strengths-based approaches simultaneously. Doing so will promote students' overall development and well-being.	Don't assume that a whole child, strengths-based approach is always easy to implement. It will require consciously doing so, and your efforts will benefit everyone.

Questions for Discussion and Reflection

- This chapter introduces the idea of a strengths-based perspective. What is it and what are some examples of it that teachers can use in the classroom?
- Draw a t-chart and contrast the two ideas: strengths-based and deficit-focused. Please write four ideas that are unique to each approach.
- What is positive psychology, and how can it contribute positively to teaching in elementary classrooms?
- What does it mean to have a whole child viewpoint? How does a strengths-based perspective coincide with a whole child approach to teaching students?

CHAPTER 10

PLANNING TO PROMOTE ALL STUDENTS' LEARNING

The perfect lesson has never been taught. When I say this to both future and veteran teachers, they respond similarly with a big sigh a relief and say, "Oh, okay, I feel better now." Why do you think they respond that way? I think it's because teachers want to do what's best for students and they are hard on themselves when lessons don't go as planned. The message implies that there's always room for improvement, which is reassuring to teachers who strive for perfection. Indeed, I've found that most teachers do. But sometimes situations come up that cannot and should not be avoided. Perhaps the fire alarm goes off at an inopportune moment, a student feels ill and needs to leave class, or students' interests take classroom inquiry in another direction. Despite knowing unexpected situations will arise, teachers need to plan for their teaching and for students' learning—to identify and think through a coherent sequence of instructional activities that will lead to student achievement.

Dear future teacher,

During my own student teaching experience, I was mentored by Ms. Gee. She wore tailored suits and buttoned-up blouses, and she meant business. She was serious about student learning. Ms. Gee planned her instruction down to the minute and expected me to do the same. Once when talking with me about teaching, she said, "Thou shalt not wing it!" Do you know what she meant? I sure did. She was telling me not to come into her classroom unprepared; her students needed and deserved much more from me than attempting to teach them without preparation. Ms. Gee taught me to value planning for instruction, and since that time, I have seen it as an essential component to teaching well and a necessity for promoting students' learning.

No winging it, okay?

K.

Many aspiring teachers find planning to teach daunting. I know it can seem overwhelming because there are multiple factors to consider simultaneously—students, objectives, standards, content, environment, vocabulary, activities, assessment, materials, questioning, and, of course, the curriculum and methods used to guide students' learning. The curriculum and methods refer to "the what and the how" of teaching. These terms describe what teachers teach and how they go about doing so and, just as teachers' personalities vary, so do their ideas about what should be taught and how it should be taught.

Beginning with the 1983 publication of *A Nation at Risk*, there has been increased national attention, focus, and scrutiny on students' academic outcomes. Questions such as the following surfaced: What should students know and be able to do upon high school graduation? What is currently being taught? Are students taught different curriculum in different locations throughout our nation, and if so, why and what are the national implications of that? Should there be a standardization of what is taught and implemented? Would students and our society be better off with standardization? Questions such as these remain common in conversations regarding educational reform, and over time, answers to these types of questions have led in part to our schooling being a standards- and outcomes-based system.

Our nation has one overarching general education law, The Elementary and Secondary Education Act (ESEA), initially passed in 1965, has a main goal of closing the education achievement gap for students growing up near and in poverty. To reach this goal, federal funding streams were established to provide financial support to schools identified as serving large populations of students from low-income families. There have been many reauthorizations of ESEA throughout the years, but one reauthorization in 2001 titled The No Child Left Behind Act (NCLB, 2001–2015), brought considerable impact to schools, teachers, and students because the funding streams became conditional based on student achievement. Under NCLB, to receive funding for their schools, states had to develop student assessments and identify a standard measure of student success. If schools repeatedly underperformed for 5 years or more, they would be penalized by the government with a mandated shutdown, or perhaps reorganized under new administration with new teachers.

While the federal government did not mandate national standards, in 2009, the National Governor's Association, a group of all 55 of our state's and territories' governors, directed the development of a set of common standards for grades K-12 to be implemented as a guide for what students should learn at each grade level. The standards were named the Common Core State Standards (CCSS) and included knowledge and skills deemed necessary for students' college and career preparation. While the CCSS were state, not federally, initiated, federal grant funding for schools was tied to adoption of CCSS. Throughout the implementation of the CCSS, 46 states adopted the standards (excluding Alaska, Nebraska, Texas, and Virginia). In most cases, the Common Core gave national direction about the content teachers should teach and when they should teach it. While the Core established learning standards, it also began to portray a national, general curriculum that teachers were required to implement. While there was considerable disagreement with many aspects related to NCLB and the associated CCSS, the standards remained in place as direction for students' curriculum throughout the 14 years of its existence.

Dear future teacher,

I began teaching in public schools in fall 1988 and left in spring 2004 for a second career in teacher preparation. Since I left public schooling before NCLB and CCSS gained strong footing in schools, I never had direct experience teaching during its implementation. I did, however, hear a lot about the experiences from my longtime colleagues who asserted that I "got out at the right time." "Oh, gosh," I thought, "how could it have gotten that bad?" As I described previously, these were my colleagues who stayed after school with me and went into school on weekends with me to plan students' activities. I wondered how the new standards could really impact teachers that negatively. Throughout the media, I read countless teachers' concerns about their perceptions of swift implementation and unrealistic content. On some occasions, I met with new teachers who explained that while teaching to the standards was one thing, they were even more troubled when provided with a scripted curriculum—at times seeming like a screenplay with what to what to say, what to do, and what to ask students—as a requirement to follow. They explained that there was no planning to do because everything had been planned and written out for them. As I listened, their trepidation became more of a reality when they showed me a detailed district-level pacing guide that pinpointed calendar dates to identify what content they were required to teach by when. The new teachers expressed concern for losing their jobs if they did not reach the deadlines. "What should I do," they asked, "when some students need more time to review what I'm teaching?" "What will I do when students express an interest in topics outside of the listed curriculum?" I was at a loss as to how to help them. On one hand, I wanted to tell them to do right by their students, to let their teaching be guided by students' needs and interests; but on the other hand, I understood their concerns about not performing as the district wanted them to and I knew that their fears of potential job loss were justified. In the end, I talked with them about the need for finding a professional balance, to try to develop a knack for knowing how far they could drift from the pacing guide before they needed to regroup and come back to it. Was that helpful? I'm not sure. Indeed, this was a dilemma that did not have a true win—win solution. The new teachers' concerns brought to mind a quote I've heard many times: "Students' education is not a one-size-fits-all kind of thing."

K.

In 2015, the No Child Left Behind Act was reauthorized again and replaced by the Every Student Succeeds Act (ESSA), which brought and will potentially continue to bring many differences to education as it is rolled out. While NCLB based substantial federal funding for schools on students' performance, ESSA does not. Instead, ESSA has been designed to specifically support (not penalize) underperforming schools. By law, ESSA will provide additional funding to help low-performing schools reach desired outcomes. In addition, ESSA shifts schools' accountability of students' outcomes from the federal level to the state level and mandates that schools' federal funding cannot be determined based on schools' and students' performance. Instead, schools will be held accountable to their states.

This essentially dismantled the informal, yet interwoven, nature of the Common Core State Standards with federal law. ESSA grants flexibility to states regarding whether or not they want to continue using the Core, and many have decided to rewrite their own learning standards. Indeed, schools continue to be in the midst of change as federal and state reform efforts continue to be implemented (ESSA, 2015).

There is a new component in the 2015 reauthorization of the federal education law that offers something quite unique to schools, teachers, and students. Embedded in ESSA is a federal endorsement of a specific teaching framework, Universal Design for Learning (UDL), which holds considerable promise for promoting all students' achievement, 2016). This federal endorsement is the first of its kind to advocate for a specific approach to planning and designing classroom instruction.

Dear future teacher,

ESSA's endorsement of UDL marks a significant shift in the focus of our federal education law, and it has significant implications for you as a future teacher and for current teachers as well. In the past, federal law focused on students' outcomes, which was a products-driven reform effort. At the federal and state levels, a school's performance was exclusively determined by students' standardized math and English language arts test scores and by high school graduation rates—outcomes represented as products of teachers' instruction. However, with ESSA endorsing a teaching framework, the scope of focus widens to encompass the teaching processes used to reach those outcomes. In that way, ESSA has the potential to broaden educational reform to bring about both process- and products-based changes. Universal Design for Learning is a framework that encompasses every aspect of teaching, and research shows that the approach promotes all students' learning (CAST, 2023). Since UDL focuses on both processes and products, it obliges teachers to focus on planning, teaching, and assessment.

K.

I'd like to tell you a metaphor that is not my own. It is quite well known in our educational literature about Universal Design for Learning and provides considerable insight into the thought processes necessary for planning and teaching all students well. It goes like this: Imagine yourself as an architect planning to construct a building. Your plans require the front door to be located well above ground level. What would you plan to construct in front of it so people could enter? Perhaps you would plan to build steps. If you did, however, you might soon realize that your building wouldn't be accessible to some. People using wheelchairs and people pushing baby strollers, for example, wouldn't be able to enter. You then realize that steps would become like a barrier to some entering your building. So then, as an afterthought, you realize that you will need to build a ramp to accommodate those who cannot use the front steps. You then notice that there is not enough room for both steps and a ramp at the entry of the front door. So you consider adding the ramp to the side or the back of the building. After additional contemplation, you don't like that idea because those who use the side or back entrances will have less of an experience than those who enter through the front door. What should you plan to do? You then realize that you can revise the plan to replace the front steps with a ramp in front of the building because the ramp can accommodate everyone. Those who can walk can easily go up the ramp, and those who use wheelchairs, crutches, and strollers can go up it as well. It's a win–win, a universal design that works for everyone. Many teachers have applied the principles mentioned in this metaphor about accessible architecture to their plans for teaching students, and they have reported much success when doing so (Jimenez et al., 2007).

I'd like to tell you about a man named Ronald Mace who was diagnosed with polio as a young child and, as a as a result, used a wheelchair throughout the rest of his life. As a college student, Mace studied architectural design and became an architect. Throughout his career, he advocated for and designed housing and buildings that were accessible for people with disabilities, promoting architectural designs that would work for all. He called his approach "universal design," which provided a framework for planning and building accessible architecture by eliminating potential barriers (Jimenez et al., 2007). In the mid-1980s, David Rose and Ann Meyer studied Mace's ideas of universal design, applied the concepts to students' learning environment, and cofounded the Center for Applied Special Technology (CAST). They, along with other staff at CAST, extended Mace's accessible architectural concepts of universal design to teaching and named their work "Universal Design for Learning" (UDL) (Jimenez et al., 2007). This is the UDL framework that is endorsed in ESSA, and as such, is one that teachers are encouraged by federal law to implement in their classrooms (CAST, 2023).

You may not know this, but in the past, teachers were taught to teach "to the middle." The idea was that teaching would work for most of the students if done this way. However, the approach actually served very few. The approach didn't offer additional challenges for those who needed it, didn't allow for supports for those who required it, and, as for a true middle, it didn't actually exist. Students' needs were not and are not met by this approach. Universal Design for Learning provides an entirely different methodology than teaching to the middle. It accounts for all learners. A UDL approach provides a way to design teaching so curriculum can be understood by all students.

The Center for Applied Special Technology (CAST) offers resources and support to apply Universal Design for Learning (UDL) approaches to teaching. CAST suggests that there are three main UDL principles that can be used to do this. CAST promotes identifying, minimizing, and eliminating barriers to learning. As a future teacher, it will be beneficial for you to use the UDL principles as a guide for your own instructional planning because the principles will provide you with direction for presenting information, engaging students in learning, and assessing what they've learned.

The first UDL principal is to portray new content by using multiple (more than one) and varied (different) representations of it. The idea is that one representation of any concept is not enough for all students to truly understand it. As an example, if I were teaching science content about cell division, I could ask students to read a description in a book about the concept, but in doing so, I would only provide students with one representation of it. Since I only offered one representation of the content, my singular teaching method would essentially act as a barrier to some students' learning because an approach that works for one will not work for all. If I provide students with additional information to read, the representation of the concept is still limited to written description; while it would provide multiple representations of the content (more than one book), it wouldn't provide varied representations of it (different resources and materials). So the question becomes, what different ways could content be presented to teach the concept? This first principle suggests that multiple and varied teaching materials such as graphics, videos, and physical models can and should be used when representing curricular information.

Dear future teacher,

Ryan's energetic spirit led him swiftly through our classroom. He barely sat still while I taught, and I did what I could to accommodate his high energy. There were times when I heard him say, "I don't get it" after I taught a lesson. Sometimes, I'll admit, I felt tired and hearing "I don't get it" seemed to make teaching seem even more exhausting. I replied, "What don't you get?" and he'd say, "I just don't get it. I don't get any of it." His statements made me feel defeated, like something got in my way of teaching him. In response to his complaints, I would scramble in my mind and throughout the classroom to find different teaching materials to represent concepts in different ways. For example, when teaching about fractions, Ryan did not understand abstract expressions such as the fractions one half or one fourth so I hustled about the classroom to find physical models of parts of a whole so he could see and hold the models himself. Not surprisingly, he understood fractions even more when I provided him with relatable representations of it such as a candy bar broken into sections to show parts of a whole. I can now see that my initial teaching method only provided abstract ideas (showing fractions as symbols on paper) so my teaching method actually got in the way of Ryan's learning. While I was teaching, I realized the need for using multiple and varied representations of new concepts by responding to "I don't get it" statements. Had I used UDL principles during my planning, I would have planned ahead to included multiple and varied representations of content during the lesson, rather than as scrambling afterthoughts to support Ryan's learning.

UDL provides direction for planning and for teaching.

K.

The second UDL principle, action and expression, includes two separate but related components. The first component, action, refers to the procedures and activities that teachers and students use to interact with new content. This describes the processing (i.e., thinking) students to do to learn new information. Just as the first principle requires multiple and varied representations of new content, this second principle requires multiple and varied actions during the lesson to ensure students' processing leads to understanding something new. When students are provided with multiple means of processing new information, they are more inclined to understand it. The second component to this principle, expression, refers to providing students with different options to show what they know. The UDL approach suggests that multiple and varied assessments such as written narratives, tests, and quizzes, as well as in-person interviews and presentations, sketched drawings, models, charts, and graphic organizers are all methods of assessment that students could use to portray new knowledge gains. The idea here is that teachers should not rely on any one means of assessment for an entire class of students all the time because not all students express their knowledge best in the same way.

The third UDL principle is referred to as engagement, suggesting teachers need to elicit student interest and motivation in learning new content. To do this, CAST recommends that teachers provide students with choices about their learning. Providing students with autonomy about what they learn is important because it can be self-motivating for students to select their own inquiry into new topics. However, this principle can be more challenging for you to implement than you may realize because curriculum is not typically flexible enough for teachers to provide students with free choices about what they learn. I know that is most unfortunate because teachers should be able to promote students' inquiry about topics that interest them, but that is not often easy to do. You see, as I mentioned previously, many school districts have an established curriculum that teachers are required to follow. So when your future students reveal their own topics of interest, it will be important that you are both willing and creative with finding multiple niches of opportunities within a provided curriculum to embed students' interests. Indeed, they will benefit from you doing so (CAST, 2023).

Universal Design for Learning offers an approach to teaching that provides students with multiple and varied options for accessing new content and motivates them to actively participate in their own learning. UDL practices recognize and use students' different backgrounds, learning preferences, strengths, needs, and abilities to design flexible, instructional activities that benefit all students. Research suggests that the UDL framework can be used to successfully plan instruction for promoting all students' learning (CAST, 2023). The touchstone for this chapter is: **Universal Design for Learning will support and promote all students' learning** (CAST, 2023). The following chart provides insight into what to do and what not do when teaching.

TOUCHSTONE FOR TEACHING: UNIVERSAL DESIGN FOR LEARNING WILL SUPPORT AND PROMOTE ALL STUDENTS' LEARNING

What to Do	What Not to Do
Take time to thoughtfully plan your instruction. While plans may change, proactively planning clear and coherent lessons is essential.	Don't skip or even minimally plan lessons. It is likely that students' learning will not be optimized if you do.
When possible, use students' backgrounds, strengths, interests, learning preferences, and challenges as the basis for lesson planning and instruction.	Don't plan for all students to do the same activities and assignments. All students are different, and they will benefit from having different options to engage with the content and express what they know.

What to Do	What Not to Do
When planning, work to identify and remove barriers that may interfere with learning. Barriers will weaken your instruction and limit students' learning.	Don't assume your teaching methods are working for all students. Most teaching includes some potential barriers that may interfere with student achievement.
Plan for and use multiple and varied materials, activities, and assessments to promote student learning.	Don't limit your instruction by only using one material or resource. Students learn differently so they will need different materials and resources to maximize their learning.
Use Universal Design as a framework for planning and instruction. Incorporate the principles of engagement, representation and action, and expression in your teaching. Doing so will support all students' learning.	Don't assume you already know about UDL principles. Studying the approach to teaching will take time and effort, but students will benefit from you doing so.

Questions for Discussion and Reflection

- What do you already know about lesson planning? What components are most familiar to you? Which are you still uncertain about?
- In this chapter, the author mentioned the overarching general education law, the Elementary and Secondary Education Act (ESEA). Describe its reauthorizations and some general shifts that have taken place since its inception.
- Why is it important to know that ESSA has endorsed UDL? What does that mean for teachers?
- Describe UDL and explain the three main components of it. Describe a lesson that has been developed using UDL principles.

Fig. 10.1. Copyright © 2013 Depositphotos/Spaces.

CHAPTER 11

LINKING LESSON PLANNING, INSTRUCTION, AND STUDENT BEHAVIOR

E very student has something important to say. Each has an individually unique perspective with unmeasurable value worth knowing and understanding. All students communicate all the time; those overly quiet and still, those excessively chatty and lively, and those who fall all along that continuum convey messages that students try to convey. As with spoken language, students' actions and behaviors are powerful forms of communication too, and it is especially important that teachers understand the messages students' behaviors portray.

In classrooms, students' behaviors are often calm and settled, but at times their actions can become disruptive to learning environments. When this happens, it can be rather upsetting to classrooms because disruptive behaviors can and usually do interrupt learning. Responses to students' disruptive behaviors vary from teacher to teacher. Indeed, there are many ideas, programs, and models that teachers use to stop, interrupt, and redirect undesirable student behaviors and keep their classrooms running smoothly. Many teachers have found that taking a proactive approach, rather than a reactive approach, to keeping students on task can be most helpful. Proactive approaches focus on preventing, not punishing, undesired behaviors. Teachers who take proactive approaches also view students' behaviors as a form of communication and perceive their actions as messages that convey needs that teachers can help to fulfill. As a future teacher, it will be important to develop proficiency with understanding students' behaviors as a form of communication and proactively planning for full student engagement. Doing so will help to establish and maintain a productive classroom learning environment so that all students' learning can be optimized.

Dear future teacher,

I think that I am quite accurate in saying that most preservice teachers I have talked with have no greater fear than a disorderly, unmanageable class. I suppose that you may also have a fair amount of fear you as you contemplate your aptitude to manage what you may refer to as "student misbehavior." I am well acquainted with that feeling because at one point, I experienced it too. I know that not having clear insight into how to manage a class or how to make sense of students' behaviors can lead to countless stressful days and sleepless nights. When I was where you are in life, approaching the entry point of my career, I didn't have much of an idea about how to design teaching and student learning in a way that could prevent unwanted student behaviors. Early in teaching, I thought that classroom management was an entirely separate entity from my planning and my teaching. But I was not right about that. In hindsight, my students would have benefited from me knowing that there is a strong connection, a tight linking, between lesson planning, teaching, and student behavior. Understanding the association these three elements have with each other will help you become proficient with managing your future classroom.

It begins with knowing what students need.

K.

Students, just like everyone, have needs that need to be met. When students enter your classroom, their physical, social, emotional, cognitive, and mental needs may or may not be met by those they live with. At the very basic level, all students need to feel and be safe physically and emotionally. They need to know and feel they are cared for and have others they care about. They need to have predictable, safe places they call home, and they need to feel and be completely free from threat and physical harm within those environments. To be prepared to learn and to be able to be fully present for learning, students need to be well rested and well fed. If and when these basic needs are not met in students' homes, chances are likely that their behaviors will in some way portray that while they are at school.

When students' basic needs are not met, their attention to learning may not be possible because physiological needs often supersede cognitive focus. Participating in classroom activities can become one of their lowest priorities as their thoughts may be overtaken with feelings of fear, hunger, and exhaustion. While often unintentional, students' focus may not be on class activities and students may communicate unmet needs with outbursts or passive withdrawal. I know it can be very challenging to identify whether students' basic needs are met so it will be important that you use keen observational skills for clues to identify it. If you find that the root cause of students' undesired behaviors is because their basic needs are not met at home, there are ways that you as a teacher can, at least in part, help to meet those needs at school. You can help by ensuring they have breakfast and lunch available to them; you can provide families with resources about housing options and effective parenting strategies and offer information about shelters and food banks if needed. And when students are in the classroom, compassionate and solution-focused listening can help. Perhaps all too often, students haven't the communication skills necessary to convey unmet basic needs so instead, they may act out. Even well-intentioned teachers may overlook their needs and impose punishments and consequences in their classrooms rather than identify why students acted as they did. It is only when teachers understand the reason behind the behavior that they can work toward helping to fulfill students' needs.

Students need to know what is expected of them and what is acceptable to those around them in their homes and classrooms. They need to know policies and rules and, just as important, they need to know why those rules are important to follow. When possible, including students in on creating rules can be a valuable, collaborative process, When students have ownership of classroom rules, it can be empowering for them to uphold them while being self-accountable to them. This process can help to foster their sense of responsibility. When students do not know the rules or do not think they matter, there is not much chance of them following the rules. Identifying this as a cause of students' unwanted behaviors is important because that can be talked about and processed together. When students know the rules and understand the reason for them, they are more likely to take ownership of them and respect them.

Inevitably, there will be times when all teachers will experience students' behaviors as less than desirable. There will be some moments when you, as a future teacher, will need to react swiftly to stop unwanted behaviors, especially if students are causing damage to their environment or emotionally or physically hurting themselves or others. There will also be times when you will be able to thoughtfully respond afterward, to reflect on and determine why they behaved as they did, and to recognize their behaviors as a form of communication. What other needs do you think students have? What messages do you think their (mis)behaviors most often convey?

Students need to feel emotionally and socially connected to others at home and at school. They need to feel liked and be liked by others. They need to feel important and that their ideas and opinions are heard, understood, and valued.

Dear future teacher,

Have you heard the saying, "Quality time spent together is more important than quantity time"? What do you think about the idea of quality time versus quantity time? Is one more important than the other or are they both important? I've found that children want time and attention, and they want plenty of both. I believe they need plenty of both too, in healthy and positive ways. When children are given the gift of attention, they feel valued and appreciated for who they are. When children are given the gift of sustained time spent with those they care about, they begin to develop a sense of self-worth. When children receive adults' time and attention in positive, affirming ways, they begin to feel important to those around them. Yet conversely, when they unfortunately do not receive the positive time and attention they need, they begin to feel unimportant and insignificant to those around them. The key is to see and hear children doing well and to draw attention to them by talking with them, listening to them, and engaging in activities with them.

Your positive time and attention will make all the difference.

K.

When teaching, you may notice some students trying to get adults' attention or the attention of their classmates by shouting out, acting silly, or even using physical actions. Their behaviors may communicate a need such as the following:

"I want to interact with you. I need to be seen and heard as important, worthwhile, and significant to you." When this happens, it is important to find ways to make personal connections with students when you're able to do so. When students try to get attention, sometimes adults respond, "She's acting that way because she wants attention. Just ignore her." Yes, the student may want (and need) attention so let's be sure to notice the moments she is doing well, when she is doing things as she ought to be doing, and call attention to her with praise and encouragement to continue. Doing so can be a strong start to fulfilling students' need for attention. Remember, if this need is not met, students' unwanted attention-getting behaviors will likely continue. Creating in-class activities that provide students with opportunities to collaborate—where classmates need each other to complete cooperative activities—is one way to fulfill students' need for attention within lesson design. Can you think of other productive ways to do so? I bet you can.

Students need to have some sense of control of their world—both at home and at school—to be able to claim ownership of it. They need to have opportunities to express their feelings, emotions, ideas, and opinions. They need to feel empowered to act in responsible ways. When students do not have occasions to make healthy choices for themselves (i.e., when choices are made for them), they can feel powerless, which can create a dependence on others. Students need to feel and be powerful, autonomous individuals in their own lives; it provides them with a sense of independence, an I-can-do-it mentality that can contribute to having ownership of their own behaviors and feeling capable when faced with situations that require decision-making and problem-solving. Students who haven't been given opportunities to develop their own sense of power may at times try to portray an unpracticed sense of it by acting powerful through physical aggression and anger either toward others or even toward themselves. As a teacher, you can guide students to shift their outward display of power over others (interpersonal) inward, so they can learn to assume their own power and use it constructively to reach their fullest potential (intrapersonal). Classroom activities that can contribute to developing students' sense of power include both individual goal-setting to reach desired targets and group collaborating to reach shared goals. Teachers can provide resources to families about helping students make smart choices for themselves and providing opportunities for meaningful decision-making at home.

Students also have a need to feel safe and secure physically and emotionally. They need to be able to fully trust that they will not be hurt by others around them at home and at school.

Dear future teacher,

When I was a child, my classmates and I used to chant, "Sticks and stones will break my bones, but words will never hurt me." The longer I've lived, the more untrue this saying has become. I know all too well that words can hurt. They can hurt a lot, can't they? I believe all of us have experienced that feeling at one point or another in our lives. The problem is that when unkind expressions are repeatedly heard, the students they are directed toward can feel left out, less than, and unwanted. These feelings can lead to despair and sadness and, more seriously, contribute to stress, anxiety, and depression. The revised saying, "Sticks and stones can break my bones, but words will hurt me too" seems truer to me, and a saying worth knowing. What can you do to create an environment where students are safe and feel safe in your classrooms?

K.

When students are hurt by others and cannot stop it from continuing, they may experience a feeling of revenge. They know they have been repeatedly harmed and have an ongoing need to protect themselves. Students may actively seek revenge and portray it as outrage and tantrums or passively as being withdrawn or sullen. Students who have been hurt may need intervention counseling and therapy outside of school to help overcome their experiences. As a teacher, you can reach out for help from support staff in your school—guidance counselors, school social workers, and school psychologists. In class, you can work toward posting predictable daily schedules so students can begin to build trust in the routines of their day, which can be a step toward trusting you. They will benefit from teacher language that is caring, supportive, and empowering. They will benefit from teachers creating "no put-downs" rules and not allowing any negative talk to enter their classroom. They will benefit most from a caring and supportive classroom community. Students need to perceive their teachers and classmates as being on their side, as allies with a "we've got your back" commitment that is both felt and experienced.

Dear future teacher,

Life can be hard. In nearly every family I've ever met, I've found that parents and caregivers want the very best for their children. It's just that life can sometimes get in the way of the best of intentions. Unexpected expenses can make families come up short on money. Unforeseen health complications can lead to job loss. Life happens and stressors can set in. How do you respond to stress? How might your response become more pronounced when young children are dependent upon you for their every need? Sometimes parents need help, and that is okay. They need everyone working together to help their students succeed.

K.

Students need to feel that they are capable—physically, socially, cognitively, emotionally, and mentally—of completing tasks at hand. When in classrooms, they need to feel confident and need to be perceived as being competent at completing activities and assignments successfully. For students to be successful in school, they need to perceive themselves as having the academic aptitude to learn and to be able to reach academic goals. When goals are too easily met, students often display no motivation to work toward them because they perceive no challenge associated with doing so. On the other hand, when students perceive goals as too difficult, they will be uninspired to work toward them too.

Russian developmental psychologist Lev Vygotsky proposed that tasks that are either too simple or too difficult do not promote students' learning. He suggested that to promote optimal learning, students need to have learning goals that are within reach, achievable with support, but not too far from students' current aptitudes so that new goals are impossible to meet. He referred to this space as the zone of proximal development. As a future teacher, you will likely have many students in your classroom, each with different zones of proximal development. The goal will be for you to design lessons that include challenging yet achievable learning goals for students and to find the just-right fit for each student. To do this, it's highly probable that you will need to plan different activities for different small groups of students so activities will fall in line within students' zones of proximal development.

When students do not believe their effort matters, they can develop apathy toward school and learning. Then, when students feel apathetic toward learning, they may resist beginning an activity, give minimal effort to completing it, or give up entirely. As a future teacher, interrupting apathy can be challenging, but redesigning some activities (when possible) that provide options for students to develop their own interests as learning goals can help to prevent it from setting in and motivate students to put forth effort to reestablish a momentum for learning.

While unfortunate, there are instances when teachers can unknowingly trigger undesired students' behaviors. For example, perhaps there is excessive downtime during a lesson; perhaps learning is set up as a sit-and-get passive experience; perhaps teachers' responses unconsciously include discouraging statements; perhaps learning materials are not readily available; or perhaps content is not clearly or coherently portrayed. Teachers can purposely plan ahead to ensure moments such as these do not happen. There are ways to plan and teach lessons that encourage and keep students on task and cooperatively interacting with classmates to learn new content. When students are actively engaged in lessons, they are more inclined to stay focused on learning and less likely to get off task.

Dear future teacher,

There's so much for you to learn about lesson plan design. I've found that a well-designed lesson can do two things at once: maximize students' learning and prevent undesired behaviors. I'd like to take a moment to tell you about a previous colleague of mine, Mrs. Paraheiter, a teacher who had what seemed to be well over 50 years teaching experience and who had the hearts of generations in the community. Mrs. P.'s classroom was not a quiet place. It was loud and busy and messy. Students constructed things. They talked together and asked each other lots of questions. They built models and solved problems cooperatively. They were active and inquisitive. One day after observing Mrs. P.'s class, I asked her, "Can you tell me about your classroom management plan? What behavior plan do you use?" Perhaps you will be surprised by what she told me. She explained, "I don't have one of those. I don't need one." And you know what? She was right; she didn't. Reflecting on Mrs. P.'s classroom kept me up at night wondering what about her teaching encouraged students to participate so actively AND stay engaged in the lesson. In retrospect, in Mrs. P.'s classroom, there was no time for students to be off task because her lesson activities required them to be on task ALL the time. Throughout the years, I've found that some teachers' management plans are, in many ways, invisible to the observer, and Mrs. P.'s classroom was an example of that. She had no interest in nor any need for systems based on sticker charts, check mark tallies, or pull-a-card, no punishment-and-reward systems, and no listed consequences. While her management plan was invisible, I can assure you that it was alive and well in her classroom. Students were on task and were learning all the time. What do you think it was about Mrs. P.'s teaching that made this possible? How do you think students perceived themselves in her classroom?

Keep thinking,

K.

When teachers know and understand students' needs and are able to identify them—basic needs for attention, power, safety, and competence (Albert, 2002)—and when teachers are also knowledgeable about how to help students meet them, they can intentionally plan lessons, participate in supportive teacher-to-student interactions and encourage caring peer-to-peer connections. All of these endeavors can work toward fulfilling students' needs while supporting them to reach their educational goals.

Dear future teacher,

Every now and then I come across authors who profoundly alter my thinking; Alfie Kohn is one of them. Kohn has written extensively about schooling, learning, teachers, and students. He changed my thinking about student behavior with his book titled Beyond Discipline: From Compliance to Community (2006). Rather than inquiring into how I could manage students' behavior with systems based on rewards and punishments, Kohn urged me to shift my thinking to question why students behave as they do in the classroom. Kohn suggested that traditional teaching and curriculum has not been set up to support students' natural self-expression, and that students get off track in classrooms because of it. He suggests that students would benefit most from teachers who focus on creating classroom communities and designing lessons that support students' natural curiosity and interaction, instead of creating extensive management plans for classroom compliance. What do you think about that?

K.

You may ask what type of lesson design can be used to work toward fulfilling students' needs? Research suggests cooperative learning structures can successfully do so because cooperative learning has been found to contribute to students' sense of belonging, increase students' self-confidence, improve and increase on-task behavior, and have embedded supports to promote students' academic outcomes (Johnson & Johnson, 2009). Cooperative learning structures are relatively easy to implement and can be used at all grade levels with all content areas and in all classrooms. Therefore, I suggest its use with lesson design because doing so will (a) facilitate students' active participation in learning; (b) strengthen students' positive social interdependence; and (c) improve students' academic outcomes.

Cooperative learning lesson design includes five variables, defined by Johnson and Johnson, as "positive interdependence, individual accountability, promotive interaction, the appropriate use of social skills, and group processing" (Johnson & Johnson, 2009, p. 366). We will look at each variable below.

Positive interdependence refers to students needing each other to complete a task within a lesson, and it is an essential component to cooperative learning. Cooperative activities require students to interact with each other in meaningful ways. As an example, students would complete a science experiment by assuming different roles to carry out; each student would need other members of the group to complete tasks to reach an identified, shared goal. Teachers often embed positive interdependence in lessons by asking students to assume different jobs within small group interactions. Doing so can contribute to students developing social skills with an "I need you and you need me" feeling, which can contribute to a sense of belonging and being needed.

When students assume roles within a small group that has an identified shared goal, the structure itself contributes to students developing a sense of individual responsibility and accountability to both their group members and to the goal being met. When individual accountability is firmly established in cooperative learning activities, it disrupts the possibility of some students not contributing to the group while others complete all the tasks. Teachers who include cooperative learning in their lesson identify ways to assess students' individual participation by ensuring that their individual roles are carried out successfully and determining students' success with reaching the shared goal.

The third and fourth variable, social interaction and appropriate use of social skills, refer to students' positively supporting each group member to complete all tasks so the shared goal can be achieved. Lessons that are designed with cooperative learning structures embed opportunities for students to provide ongoing feedback to support each other. Students' social skills can vary widely, and cooperative learning is dependent upon students' aptitude with them. While you may be inclined to identify social skills with words such as "cooperation" and "responsibility," I've discovered that those terms are quite conceptual in nature and many students are not certain of the many different and individual social skills inherent in them. Therefore, it can be most useful to consider social skills quite simply as talking, listening, taking turns, following directions, and accepting constructive feedback, for example. Teachers who design lessons using cooperative learning often find it helpful to identify one or two social skills that students may need to improve and create cooperative activities to develop them throughout a lesson. I've heard some teachers suggest that their entire rationale for using cooperative learning is to develop students' social skills because, in doing so, they contribute to their own classroom running more smoothly while simultaneously preparing students to interact positively in the larger society and to meet academic goals.

The fifth variable, group processing, refers to students communicating how they and their group members performed individually and as a group to meet the shared goal. Group processing is a learned activity, and teachers who implement cooperative learning have found it most beneficial to model and guide students to learn how to respectfully discuss each other's group contributions. While students are encouraged to be honest when discussing group members' participation, they are also encouraged to offer feedback in positive, helpful ways. Discussing what went well during learning and what may be improved upon in the future is an important skill for students to learn because it can promote self-monitoring that can lead to students' self-desired improvement.

Cooperative learning has been widely implemented by teachers throughout our world, and its success has been well documented as an effective way to simultaneously promote students' positive academic and behavioral outcomes (Johnson & Johnson, 2009). It offers teachers and students a win–win.

Dear future teacher,

This chapter included information about students' behaviors and the importance of seeing undesirable behaviors as forms of communicating needs that, when filled, can help to create a positive learning experience for all. It provided information about teachers acting proactively to recognize when students' basic needs may not be met—to realize their need for attention, for feeling powerful in their own lives, for feeling safe, and for being and being seen as competent. This chapter portrayed some solutions for fulfilling students' needs while planning, teaching, and implementing cooperative learning lessons that can benefit all students.

K.

There are many ways to solve—or at least alleviate—student behavior you may identify as undesirable. The solution, more often than not, resides in identifying students' needs and fulfilling them when you can, as well as encouraging others to join you in the effort. The touchstone for this chapter is: **Promote students' success through cooperative learning and understanding students' behavior.** (Johnson & Johnson, 2009). The following chart provides insight into what to do and not do when teaching.

TOUCHSTONE FOR TEACHING: PROMOTE STUDENTS' SUCCESS THROUGH COOPERATIVE LEARNING AND UNDERSTANDING STUDENTS' BEHAVIOR

What to Do	What Not to Do
Recognize student behavior as a form of communication.	Don't think that student behavior is random. Students' behavior is often tightly linked to unmet needs.
Analyze student behavior as needs to be fulfilled, rather than problems that require punishments to correct.	Don't rely on punishments and consequences to resolve students' undesirable behavior. Doing so will not lead to long-term change.
Support students to see themselves as being fully capable. It will help them develop a positive self-perception.	Don't assume students perceive themselves as being capable. Students need to be taught they have a boundless capacity to learn.
Plan for students to engage in cooperative learning activities. Doing so will provide opportunities for students to develop prosocial behaviors while simultaneously working toward reaching academic goals.	Don't presume that students' behaviors are not, at times, related to your planning and teaching. Teaching to fulfill students' needs while promoting academic achievement will be a win–win for you and for students.

Questions for Discussion and Reflection

- What are your thoughts about classroom management and student behavior? How well prepared do you perceive yourself to be about this topic?
- What are students' basic needs? What student behaviors might teachers notice when they are not met? How can teachers help to fulfill them?
- How might a teacher fulfill a student's need for attention when there are many other students in the class also needing to be noticed?

- Why is it important to identify students' behaviors as a form of communication? What benefits would doing so have for students and their families?
- Why would cooperative learning be a proactive solution for meeting students' needs and contributing to positive student behaviors? What might be some challenges in implementing it? How could it be successfully done?

PART 5

What We Teach

■ CHAPTER 12

TEACHING FOR SOCIAL JUSTICE

Dear future teacher,

When you become a teacher, I'm sure you will discover many teachable moments, those large and small occasions that bring about unplanned topics that can be used as opportunities for students to learn something new. Teachable moments can come and go in an instant. Sometimes teachers act on them, and sometimes they do not. Over the years, some teachable moments seemed to elbow their way into my curriculum as though they were alive and clambering for immediate attention. I'd like to share one that I experienced in a kindergarten classroom.

Brett was big for his age, yet emotionally young. He seemed to enjoy school and was eager to enter into play. One day very early in the school year, I was caught by surprise when Brett said to me, "I like playing with Sarah and Olivia and Nicole, but I don't like playing with Tonyia." I asked, "What makes you say that?" and Brett said, "Because Tonyia has dark skin and I only like to play with kids with light skin." I immediately responded, "It is not okay to say that." He didn't say a word afterward and walked away. I knew my abrupt response felt harsh to him. Did I respond in the right way? While I thought I had, something in my mind and heart felt very unsettled. The truth is, I wasn't prepared to respond to a teachable moment about racial differences, and I wanted—and needed—my response to offer more to Brett, to the other students, and especially to Tonyia.

That night and throughout the days that followed, I researched information from organizations such as Teaching Tolerance (now called Learning for Justice) to plan lessons and identify children's book titles about race and racial identity. I selected photographs of children from around the world who portrayed a beautiful continuum of skin tones to use in my lessons. I thought of Brett's words while I planned, and along with those memories came the same piercing sting I felt when I first heard them. When implementing the lessons about racial differences, I began with the pictures of the children and read nonfiction children's books that explained that skin tone differences are based on melanin and on the geographic origins of our ancestors. As the lessons progressed, I included discussions of attitudes about differences. I explained, "Children often say, 'I don't like it' or 'it's weird' when they see something that's new to them." I used language I learned from Teaching Tolerance resources and said, "When you don't know a lot about something, instead of saying you don't like it or it's weird, you could say, 'That's new to me. I don't know a lot about that yet.'" During lessons, students worked in pairs and in small groups so they had opportunities to get to know each other personally. Because they were young, I didn't know how much information they would take away from the lessons. However, over time, they began to make comments such as, "All kids can play," and "My skin color is different than your skin and that's okay," and "Some things about kids are different and some things are the same," and "I will stick up for you if someone says something mean to you." Although I knew that they still had a lot of learning to do, I felt proud of them for articulating the importance of advocacy in their own 5-year-old way, especially when they said they would stand up for each other if someone else said or did something hurtful.

I wanted to share this experience with you because it illuminates what we all probably don't want to admit—the troubling yet truthful realization that even our youngest school-age children are not immune to both portraying and experiencing racism. My hope and intention is that all future teachers will be able to confidently and productively guide students through difficult conversations such as this one. Please do what you can to prepare yourself for that challenge.

K.

I think people become uncomfortable when I say teaching is a political act, but I really see it that way. I perceive it in everything teachers do, every day, all the time. I hope I don't seem off-putting when I tell you that but I think it's especially important for you, as a future teacher, to understand what I mean. Please stay with me so I can explain. Just like most professionals, teachers need to make many choices every day. However, there is one very distinguishable way teachers' jobs are quite different than all others: unlike other professionals, teachers not only make choices that lead to task completion, but they make choices that pertain to—and influence—the thinking, perceptions, beliefs, ideals, and values of young people. You probably already realize this, but I want to be sure you know that when I said teaching is a political act, I was not referring to teachers' participation in politics or political parties. Instead, I made that comment to illuminate the influential effects teachers' perspectives and beliefs have on their students, especially when interacting with them and when portraying people, social groups, and events that pertain to our society and our world.

Dear future teacher,

I've always found the idea of a microcosm most intriguing because it defines and describes something as a complete miniature version of something larger than itself. In many ways, I think schools are microcosms of our much larger society. This idea can be useful when discussing our nation's school demographics because schools have the same characteristics as our society's population. I mean that our society's social groups—race, class, gender, religion, ability, language, sexual orientation, culture, and ethnicity—are similarly represented in our schools. As such, some of the most pervasive challenges our society's people experience regarding inequities within each social group are likewise experienced among school children. If you could hear my thinking, you'd be able to pick up on me asking you, why do you think social inequities exist? How can we work together to ensure everyone gets what we all need? Can we create a peaceful and socially just society, where all have equal access to and opportunities for resources, services, and education so everyone can reach their fullest potential? I wonder, maybe this goal would be easier to accomplish if we began in a microcosm and worked our way outward. If we were able to create socially just schools that offer all of the ideals of social justice to students, do you think the outcomes could and perhaps would ripple into our larger society? Would that be possible? Or would it be easiest to start in classrooms instead, in our tiniest microcosms, and work our way outward from there?

Do you think we could at least do that?

K.

I suspect you've heard of the idea of social justice before now so you probably bring some preconceived notions of it along with you as you're reading. One of the frequent concerns about social justice and its applicability to schooling is that, even with considerable attention given to it, it's often misunderstood because of its varied definitions and understandings (Neito, 2009). Social justice refers to all people being treated fairly and impartially so access to opportunities, resources, and services can be fully available to everyone. *Teaching for social justice* refers to an education that acknowledges the social inequities people experience and, most importantly, teaches students not to recreate the unjust world in which we live but to conceive and develop a new world for all—one that liberates all people to know and experience their own and others' inherent dignity and worth, free from prejudice, bias, and oppression so that all people have full access and opportunities to reach their grandest potential.

Marilyn Cochran-Smith, a respected scholar in the area of social justice, describes social justice as a broad, comprehensive framework as

> one that actively address[es] the dynamics of oppression, privilege, and isms, [and recognizes] that society is the product of historically rooted, institutionally sanctioned stratification along socially con- structed group lines that include race, class, gender, sexual orientation, and ability [among others]. ... Working for social justice in education means guiding students [and often being guided by students] in critical self-reflection of their socialization into this matrix of unequal relation- ships and its implications, analysis of the mechanisms of oppression, and the ability to challenge these hierarchies. (in Sensoy & DiAngelo, 2009, p. 350)

Cochran-Smith's framework references the complex undercurrents that reside in and among our society's social groups and, just as importantly, refers to the need for being reflective and introspective of social inequities so we can confront and challenge their existence.

For decades, scholars and teacher educators have included various forms of social justice initiatives in teacher preparation programs to prepare future teachers like yourself to remedy our nation's academic achievement gaps most predominantly noted between White students and students of color and students from higher and lower income families (Cochran-Smith, 2004). Despite these efforts, during the last 50 years, we have actually seen very little change in the academic outcomes between White students and students of color (Hanushek, 2016). While future teachers have often learned the importance of social justice education, why haven't we seen a change in the achievement gap so many have attempted to close? While some teachers were taught about social justice education in education classes, systematically including it in public schools has been sporadic; national policies for implementing a socially just curriculum and social justice standards have not been fully mandated nor established. Perhaps you are asking the same question that often keeps me up at night: Why haven't we made a significant change, and what can we do about it now?

Lisa Delpit, an award-winning author and scholar, suggests that students' self-perception often informs their cognitive development. In her book, *"Multiplication Is for White People": Raising Expectations for Other People's Children*, she asserts that students of color learn they are unworthy of or unable to achieve the same goals as White students not as overt messages, but implicitly from our larger society. She describes that students of color come to believe and accept implicit, disparaging oppressive messages as truths about themselves and others in their culture, and their learning becomes internalized, not just as what they know, but as who they are and who they foresee themselves to become (Delpit, 2013).

As a future teacher, you will have opportunities to interrupt students' oppression by modeling and fostering positive social interactions among your students and by valuing, encouraging, and modeling a positive, supportive affective disposition—including antibias attitudes and behaviors and appreciation of others, especially students of marginalized groups, primarily our Black and Brown students.

Dear future teacher,

As Lisa Delpit suggests, not all students will come to your classroom thinking favorably of themselves. Even at a very young age, some students will have already acquired a negative self-image and have their heads full of discouraging, defeating self-talk. A professor I once had encouraged our class to establish discourse

guidelines she referred to as Classroom Norms, which listed agree-
ments we made to guide our actions and interactions during class.
The norm we created and revisited most often was, "No put-downs
of self or others." This norm was powerful and useful, not because
we called on it when classmates put each other down (because we
didn't), but because of the extraordinary number of times we used
it to interrupt negative self-talk and self-discouraging comments
during classroom conversations. While this norm is not a comprehensive way to eliminate the deep hold of self-oppression and
oppression in general, "No put-downs of self or others" is a small
but necessary baby step. Will you give it a try in your future classroom? I hope you do.

K.

To work toward closing the achievement gap, future teachers like yourself will need to keenly watch and listen for bias and oppression (it exists in every school), and work toward eliminating it by ensuring that all students, especially students of color, are seen and see themselves as equally worthwhile. Just as importantly, they will need you to help them unlearn the negative implicit bias they may have accepted as "truth" and reteach them about their individual and collective inherent dignity and worth.

Attempting to remove bias from teaching and from classrooms is not new. You may have heard it referred to as antibias teaching and, although not policy driven (although I would suggest it ought to be), many schools and teachers have implemented it for years. Delpit suggests that while curriculum needs to be bias-free, there is also an important need for teachers to deeply understand the cultural histories that Black and Brown students and all students of color have assumed as part of their identities and as such, bring it with them into their classrooms, schools, and society (2013).

To prepare for understanding students' cultural histories, it is often helpful for future teachers to begin to self-identify their own social identities, cultural histories, and related biases (of self and others) and work toward understanding how their perceptions and expectations of students could and do influence their own students' academic achievement (Dover, 2009). How would you describe your own cultural history? What about your social identity? What biases do you have?

Research suggests even the most introspective teachers may have difficulty self-identifying their own negative biases because some forms of bias reside uncon-sciously in thinking and in portrayal (Staats, 2015). Unconscious, implicit bias, unless discovered, exposed, and disrupted, may unintentionally inform your future choices and instructional decision-making, which could lead to detrimental effects on your future students' learning. Understanding the notion of implicit bias may assist you with some self-discoveries of it.

Implicit bias is often noted in teachers' language when interacting with students and responding to student behavior. Did you ever notice or experience negative bias portrayed by any of your previous teachers? Knowing about the wide spectrum of biases—ranging from implicit and subtle to explicit and obvious—can help you work toward ensuring it doesn't become part of your own future teaching and students' learning.

Perhaps it's easiest to begin identifying negative implicit biases by considering some common classroom interactions where bias has often been found to occur. For example, let me start by asking you questions related to gender: Were you ever in a class where boys participated more often than girls? Did you ever have a teacher who gave more attention (either negative or positive) to boys than girls? Were you ever in a class where boys dominated discussions? If you answered yes to any, some, or all of these three questions, chances are that you witnessed some form of negative gender bias in your previous educational experiences. When you considered answers to the questions I posed, perhaps you thought, "Well, most males just talk more than females" or perhaps you thought, "Males are just more active than females so they would naturally get the most attention." Responses such as these are examples that portray implicit gender bias (Lundeberg, 1997). These examples portray beliefs about gender differences (overgeneralizing and stereotyping ways males and females act and interact) that lead to subconscious "truths" in thought, in portrayal, and in action. Prospective teachers, such as yourself, who come to teacher preparation programs with thoughts such as these should not self-blame because such beliefs arise from years of cultural influence. However, it is essential that as a prospective teacher, you learn about and discover your own negative biases (we all have them) and work toward eliminating them before becoming a teacher. It is important that you do so because your personal beliefs will inform your professional teaching practices and negative bias can and will inform your decision-making about your teaching, students, and curriculum. The goal is to ensure that you develop antibias teaching language, policies, and practices because doing so is essential if you are to provide equitable educational experiences for all students.

It is well documented that teachers who hold negative stereotypical views about differences among race, class, gender, and culture may often create inequitable motivation, experiences, and outcomes for students, especially Black and Brown students and students of low socioeconomic status (Dover, 2009). When situations such as these arise, students of such marginalized groups are not provided with equitable learning experiences or achievement opportunities, which can adversely impact their self-expectations and sense of academic competencies (Dover, 2009).

As you can probably imagine and may have even experienced yourself, these conditions can be exacerbated when observed by other students because they may perceive unjust actions and treatment as tolerable, acceptable, and "normal." It is for these reasons that aspiring teachers like yourself need to be well aware of and competent with implementing socially just teaching practices.

As I mentioned in a previous chapter, statistics on today's teacher demographics suggest that most are White, middle-class females, which is very different than the increasing multicultural student population across our nation. The National Center for Education Statistics reported that since 2014, "less than half of the public-school students have been white" and nearly 20% of school-age children now live in poverty (McFarland et al., 2019). The demographic divide between teachers and students can be potentially problematic because teachers may enter their classroom knowing very little about cultures other than their own, which can lead to making false assumptions about students' home cultures. Those assumptions can lead to forming biases. While some forms of bias can be favorable, this is most often not the case, and when considering differences among social groups and racial bias, most is unfavorable toward the "other." Learning who your students are—truly discovering who they are completely free from any unfavorable biases and stereotyping that you may have—is necessary to genuinely support and encourage their development.

Dear future teacher,

I know you won't want to believe that you have negative biases and stereotypes, but it's important to contemplate that likelihood. I bet you'd like a quick fix to eliminate any negative bias you discover, but that is not really possible. It will take time, introspection, and interactions with others to do so. Sometimes I've heard people describe racial bias as the elephant in the room—a huge problem that we are all aware of but no one really feels comfortable enough acknowledging and discussing. The truth is that we so desperately need teachers who are willing to openly and honestly talk about all forms of biases— especially racial bias—so that we can all work toward eliminating it. It is only when we name it and talk about it that we can truly work toward eliminating it in schools. We need teachers who perceive, interact with, and teach all students in equitable and equally favorable ways, and eliminating racial bias is one way for that to happen.

Who in your own life could you talk with about these ideas?

K.

Although I previously mentioned that self-identifying negative bias can be difficult for teachers to do, the good news is that there is some evidence to show that prospective teachers can be taught to self-identify, interrupt, and change unfavorable stereotypes and bias to work toward creating classrooms that include equitable experiences and opportunities for all students (Lundeberg, 1997). The National Association for Multicultural Education (NAME) is an organization that advocates for teaching for social justice and offers resources and services for promoting multicultural education and equity in schools and classrooms. NAME advocates for the use of practical and applicable resources, including questions and scenarios that can help teachers self-identify bias while working toward developing equitable teaching practices. Some of NAME's questioning to teachers (and a few that can get you started now) include, "How can my assumptions influence how I see and interact with people in negative ways?" and "How can I be more aware of my own implicit bias?" (NAME, 2019). Such questioning is a good starting place for inquiring into your own perceptions and beliefs about others who are dissimilar to you.

Delpit asserts, "We live in a society that nurtures and maintains stereotypes ... What are we really doing to better educate poor children and children of color? ... What should we be doing? The answers, I believe, lie not in a proliferation of new reform programs but in some basic understanding of who we are and how we are connected and disconnected from one another" (1995, pp. xiii–xv). Delpit's suggestion that we understand how we are connected to and disconnected from one other is a topic we don't often talk about every day, at least not in deep, thoughtful reflection. What do you think we would discover if we were to do so?

To maximize your future students' learning, you will need to be able to connect with them (i.e., relate to them). To do so, you will need to know and understand their cultural histories, especially students from marginalized cultures and races. I say this because cultural histories reveal struggles and triumphs, both collectively and individually. Students' histories inform their identities. Your future students will have very diverse histories that are derived from both personal experiences and ancestral heritage. Some students' histories will have afforded them with experiences full of societal privilege and power, while other students' experiences will have been full of disadvantage and oppression. The goal is to recognize and learn who your students are by understanding the many experiences they bring with them into your future classroom so you can truly know their perspectives, what they value, and what they need and be informed about how to teach them best.

Dear future teacher,

when I was a doctoral student, I participated in a program called the Future Professoriate Project, which offered regularly scheduled workshops about how to teach in diverse classrooms. A few of the workshops focused on revealing power structures within social groups. At that time, it was a topic I hadn't previously considered, and I found it very interesting to participate in discussions with other students from all around the world, including places such as Kenya, Korea, China, Saudi Arabia, India, and the United States. At the start of one of the workshops, we were asked to identify ways people are diverse and just as you might expect, we came up with a list that included race, class, gender, religion, ability, nationality, language, sexual orientation, culture, and ethnicity. The instructor then asked us to identify which subgroups within each of these classifications have power in our society and which do not. At first, there was some hesitancy about how to begin so the instructor explained that the subgroups with power would be those who are highly influential over others, those who have a greater ability to control their own and others' outcomes than those who do not. we started discussing socioeconomic differences and, quite universally, we agreed that those who are in the upper class have more power in our society than those who are not. we discussed ideas of power broadly and came to a shared understanding that words that ended with -ism (racism, classism, sexism, for example) were terms that described a belief that favors one subgroup over another. For example, having a belief that males are better than females at any given task would be an example of sexism; white over non-white would be an example of racism. we also came to a mutual understanding that oppression referred to the unjust treatment of those without power, especially when controlled by those who held a bias or prejudice against them. The conversation led to understanding that power structures are not the same from culture to culture and it was important to understand the power structures specific to the culture in which we teach.

Near the end of the discussion, the facilitator asked, "which social subgroups have power in our society?" Our answer revealed that those with power were white, upper-class, Christian males who are English speaking, able bodied, able minded, and heterosexual. we concluded with the realization that, just as in society, inequitable power structures can and often do exist in classrooms and as teachers, we can and should work toward creating learning activities that balance power among students because in doing so, all students would have opportunities to experience equitable education practices. We also came to recognize the importance of thoughtfully planning our teaching to ensure that all students' voices are equally heard and to ensure the use of carefully selected antibias teaching materials. I ask you this: Do you think you can work toward developing equity-oriented teaching practices? Why would it matter?

K.

Classrooms cannot and will not become places that are equity-oriented on their own. To truly create a socially just learning environment, it takes teachers and students working together, with deliberate and consistent attention given to all the interactions that happen within their shared space—school policies, educational materials and practices, language, classroom rules, and personal interactions. Talking about differences and diversity and discussing the attitudes and perceptions associated with them is important not only when they arise as teachable moments, but as purposefully selected focus woven throughout daily conversations, as normal and expected discussion topics.

Perhaps you have heard students use biased language in schools. Indeed, a lot of it is used and heard by students throughout our nation. Expressions such as "That's so gay" have become normalized as a common descriptor by many of today's young people. For students who are not heterosexual, that phrase is often hurtful because it's used to reference something unpleasant, unwanted, and flawed. When students who identify as gay hear others use the word "gay" to describe something that's disgraceful, they are apt to apply those negative connotations to their own self-identities. Students who identify as lesbian, gay, bisexual, and transgendered (LGBTQ+) regularly report experiencing discrimination, bullying, and harassment in schools. Overwhelmingly, statistics suggests that LGBTQ+ youth are at risk for substance abuse and suicide far more than their heterosexual classmates (Almeida, et al., 2009). While there are no current national education policies in place to support equities of LGBTQ+ students in schools (I believe there should be to), over one third of our states have laws that prohibit bullying students on the basis of sexual orientation and gender identity. While this is a start, it's important to note that currently at least eight states in our country have laws in place that restrict teachers from discussing LGBTQ+ issues altogether (Human Rights Campaign, 2018). If teachers can't talk about issues LGBTQ+ students experience, how can they help support their learning? Teachers need to be able to discuss all ways people are diverse and need the freedom to challenge biased language by explicitly stating that students should not to use it and explaining why not to use it and why not to accept its use by peers. Teachers also need to take time to deconstruct biased language to explain the implicit messages it conveys. Challenges such as these can be difficult, however, because it means teachers need to confront their own biases to ensure their teaching and classrooms portray equitable care, respect, and opportunities toward all students, with the goal of all students reaching their fullest potential.

Biased language can take many forms, and sometimes you may hear it as part of jokes about differences as well. Many Muslims and Jews have been on the receiving end of others making jokes about their religious differences. Jokes of this nature need to be challenged and stopped. When jokers are confronted, they are often quick to retort, "I didn't mean it. Can't you take a good joke?" But jokes about religious differences are publicly and personally offensive. They sarcastically insult personal, cherished faiths. Overhearing jokes about religious diversity are examples of teachable moments. How would you respond? Please keep in mind that all biased language is disrespectful, insulting, and hurtful, and it can and will negatively impact students' learning. Your proactive response to stop it can and will make a difference with your students' achievement.

While students learn by interacting with others, they also learn by reading, listening, and viewing educational resources and materials. As a future teacher, it will be important for you to use caution and discretion when selecting students' resources to ensure they are multicultural, antibias, and free from stereotyping. Teaching materials need to represent differences in others, including all the ways people are diverse. I encourage you to knowledgeably select the books students read, which posters you display, and which media you choose to show. While choices about books, posters, and media may seem innocuous to you, the reality is that none of it will come without influence. If your teaching materials only portray one culture or race, your teaching materials will promote one culture or one race over another—and those choices can and will implicitly and explicitly influence students' learning about themselves and others. All students need to see and hear positive models that they can relate to so they can identify qualities they believe they can realistically develop in themselves. If students do not see others similar to themselves represented in educational materials, they will learn implicitly that people who look like them or sound like them are insignificant and not worthy of attention, and unfortunately, they can and will generalize that learning onto themselves.

Our school children experience no greater burden and pain than social inequities (Delpit, 1995). Social justice is an ideal to continually strive toward in our classrooms, schools, and society. It requires us all to be fully engaged in an active participatory process of discovery. This chapter offers a very small glimpse into contemplating how to teach in a way that can create a socially just classroom. I hope you'll join me in this journey. I know the effort will be worth it. The touchstone to take away from this chapter is this: **Teaching for social justice will promote students' learning** (Cochran-Smith, 2004; Delpit, 2013). If you were to teach for social justice, what would you do? What wouldn't you do?

TOUCHSTONE FOR TEACHING: TEACHING FOR SOCIAL JUSTICE WILL PROMOTE STUDENTS' LEARNING

What to Do	What Not to Do
Acknowledge that bias, prejudice, and stereotyping exist in all schools and classrooms and work toward identifying it and eliminating it. Doing so will provide greater opportunities for students to learn.	Don't think you are bias and prejudice free. These dispositions are learned, but they can be unlearned as well.
Analyze your own past to identify your self-identity, cultural history, and biases. Knowing yourself can be a starting place when creating a socially just classroom.	Don't make assumptions about students' home lives and cultures. Take time to get to know students' families, their histories and cultures. Doing so will help you to facilitate their learning.
Help students learn and appreciate the many ways others are diverse.	Don't overlook ways students are different. Each has ways they are individually unique.
Teach about implicit and explicit bias and stereotyping and ways that it hurts everyone. Doing so will be a step toward helping it stop.	Don't assume your teaching and educational materials are free from bias. It can take careful scrutiny to identify and select antibias learning resources.
Infuse antibias lessons within currently existing curriculum and in teachable moments when they arise.	Don't let biased language go by unchallenged. When you hear negative, disparaging comments, address them head-on and encourage others to stop saying them.
Develop a strength with implementing social justice teaching practices as a normal, recurring part of your job.	Don't presume teaching for social justice won't make a difference. Supportive and antibiased language and actions can be very influential and students will learn from your modeling and replicate what you say and do.

Questions for Discussion and Reflection

- Describe your own culture. How is your culture different from that of your classmates? How is it similar?
- In this chapter, the author introduced us to Brett, a kindergarten student who said, "I don't want to play with Tonyia because she has dark skin. I only like to play with kids with light skin." If you were the teacher, how would you respond to this situation in the moment? What longer range plans would you create?
- How does the author define social justice? How might a socially just classroom look? What would you see? What would you hear?
- Why does teaching for social justice matter? Who benefits from it and how do they benefit from it?

CHAPTER 13

TEACHING TO PROMOTE SOCIAL AND EMOTIONAL LEARNING

A s students progress through school, they will learn how to read and how to write, how to count and how to solve all sorts of equations. They will also learn about our histories and about the physical world in which we live. While each academic area of study is essential, it is equally important for students to learn how to get along with others, how to be kind, caring, and thoughtful, to understand different perspectives, and to develop the capacity for compassion and empathy. Students need to learn how to ask for help and how to receive it and how to care for others and be cared for. Students do not live in this world alone, and they, as well as others around them, will at some point come up against challenges that life will inevitably bring their way. When that happens, it will be important for all students to be able to efficaciously respond to it. These are the fundamental ideals of social and emotional learning, and research in this area has shown a strong connection between students' social and emotional aptitude and their academic success. In other words, the stronger students are with being aware of their own emotions and knowing how to proactively respond to the emotions of others—while also comfortably and respectfully interacting with them—the stronger students' academic performance will be. Why do you think this is so?

When students have a strong social network around them, they have many opportunities to ask for and receive help. This, in turn, provides them with more opportunities to be successful. In addition, when students are part of a strong social community, they have many opportunities to be helpful. When students are helpful, they contribute to others, which leads them to their feeling individually worthwhile. These social experiences foster students' sense of value and connectedness with others, providing a foundation for their future social and academic success.

At first, it may seem that emotion and cognition are not associated with each other, but that is not true. Research on cognition suggests that emotions play an important part in learning. "We know emotion is important in education—it drives attention, which in turn drives learning and memory" (Sylwester, 1994, p. 60). Emotions can impact students' learning in favorable and unfavorable ways. Emotions such as excitement and joy can swiftly pull students into learning, while emotions such as fear, loss, and sadness can have them quietly withdraw or angrily act out. Emotions are universal—but our responses to them are not. Students need to learn how to manage and respond to their feelings in healthy, productive ways. This requires students to be self-aware, to know their own feelings, and to understand their responses to them.

Helping students develop a sense of self-awareness begins by guiding them toward noticing their own feelings, behaviors, and attitudes. Some students are willing to talk about themselves in this way, but others will need guided support and encouragement to do so. When students are self-aware, they are able to identify and connect their experiences and/or thinking to their feelings. This can also help them to self-manage their behaviors. For example, students who can connect an angry feeling to their associated experience can reflect on what caused the feeling and work toward shifting their thinking about it, which can elicit a different, more comfortable emotion. It is the students' thinking about their experiences (i.e., their interpretations about what happened) that will elicit their emotions. This thinking plays a very important role in being self-aware. It also plays an important role in students' self-management. Students display competence with being self-aware when they are to be able to trace their feelings back to events and their thinking that caused them. This is an especially important skill; when students rethink their interpretations of what happened, they have the ability to choose an empowering way to interpret the events. Without this self-awareness, they do not.

Dear future teacher,

Erin was in my second-grade class while her parents were in the middle of a messy divorce. Her parents each wanted full custody of Erin, which put her into a push-and-pull situation that was devastating to Erin and disheartening to me. Erin had a lot of feelings that needed to be thought through, even if just for herself. Erin's learning was often interrupted by her sadness. It was difficult for her to be attentive in class when her emotions pulled her attention elsewhere. I started a Feelings Journal with her so she could write or draw to describe her emotions. I think we all need something like that sometimes—to have a way to get some of our feelings outside of ourselves. Erin's journal helped her a lot with that. Sometimes she would share it with me. One time I read an entry where she wrote, "I am very, very, very, very, very sad because my parents are getting divorced." Her "verys" went clear across the page. She had drawn a picture of her family with her dad along the far-left side, her mom to the far right, and her standing alone crying in the middle. How do you think I should have responded? I could have ignored it. I could have told her not to feel so sad, but instead, I decided to talk openly with Erin about her sadness, to acknowledge the feelings she had. I said something like, "Erin, I know you are sad and what is happening makes me feel sad too." I then waited quietly. She looked up with a slight smile. I think that acknowledging feelings is important because it portrays a message that it is okay to feel as you do; it validates both the feelings and the individual who has them. Somehow, doing so lessened the load for Erin. I think it helped her to feel that she was not alone, and I believe she felt much comfort knowing that.

K.

Research on social and emotional learning (SEL) suggests that there are many benefits of students developing a strong self-awareness of their emotions, including developing confidence, self-efficacy, a growth mindset, and resiliency—the belief that life's challenges can be overcome (CASEL, 2021). Research on SEL also portrays the importance of students developing an aptitude with self-management. Self-management refers to students' abilities to control their behaviors associated with emotions (responses and reactions) and to manage them in healthy, productive ways.

Emotional stability helps students become successful socially and academically. While students will have many different experiences that will elicit different emotions, it is how they self-manage them that is important to their success socially and academically. Self-management can help students be in control and stay in control of their behaviors. As I mentioned before, we all respond to emotions differently. That means you will have students in your class who will respond to emotions differently. Some will do so quietly, some will want to talk all about it, and others may respond with verbal and physical outbursts. Self-managing emotions can be challenging for some students, but teachers can assist with learning that management. Teachers can guide students to use simple techniques such as counting down to discharge anger, taking a deep breath before acting impulsively, or thinking through a challenging situation to find a solution that works for all. Research suggests that one of the most common feelings students have in school is stress, and it is especially important that teachers understand it and that students learn healthy ways to manage it.

Dear future teacher,

Students need to know that emotions are a normal part of life. There are many times when emotions will make them feel happy, sad, angry, fearful, and joyful. Sometimes, emotions can feel very strong and overwhelm students, which can cause feelings of stress. Stress can bring many harmful consequences along with it, including anxiety, depression, and heart and health problems. Even our youngest students are susceptible to its negative impact. It's important to watch for signs of stress that students might portray, such as changing behaviors, having difficulty focusing, acting out, or withdrawing socially. I'd like to tell you about one way a middle school teacher I know helps her students learn to identify and manage stress. As a culminating project for a unit on emotions, the teacher asks students to create fictional animal characters and write a children's book portraying how they overcome a stressful situation (divorce, bullying, or family illness, for example) by using self-management strategies to do so. One of the most meaningful aspects of the project comes after students have completed their stories. They take their books into elementary classrooms to read and talk about their stories with younger students. In this way, the project requires the middle schoolers to give deeper contemplation into how to talk about different coping strategies they portray, while simultaneously teaching young children how to manage their own stress. Indeed, a win—win when promoting social and emotional learning.

K.

Students are growing up in an increasingly diverse world. They need to learn how to get along with others, to understand differences, and to relate to others in respectful, supportive, and productive ways. They need practice developing strong relationship skills so they can contribute to their own growth and the growth of others. Relationship skills are an essential component of social and emotional learning that includes respectfully interacting with others and supportively responding in kind and caring ways (CASEL, 2021).

Inherent to relationship skills is the ability to communicate with others—a collaborative weaving together of listening, speaking, reading, writing, and gesturing to convey ideas. Teachers can help build students' relationship skills by providing them with opportunities to communicate with each other. Students can interact with teachers to ask questions, express what is known, and explain their thought processes aloud. Research has revealed time and again that learning is a social activity and that student interaction plays a big part in it (Dewey, 1963). Prospective teachers need to be aware, however, that some research has found that, despite being in close proximity with each other, student-to-student communication is not something that is always observed in classrooms. Rather, studies have found that it is quite common for teachers to do most of the talking themselves (Goodlad, 1984). Students learn to communicate by communicating, and it is important to provide students with many opportunities to engage in it.

Dear future teacher,

Have you ever contemplated the number of paired combinations that can be made in a classroom? I believe it's not something teachers always think about, but I encourage you to do so because it can illuminate the many different paired social interactions that exist in students' learning environments. Let me provide you with an example to show you what I mean. Let's say that you have a very small class of four students, including Tina, Jacob, Leandra, and Hyo. How many different paired combinations could exist among them? Perhaps it's more than you'd initially think. There would be six including: Tina and Jacob, Tina and Leandra, Tina and Hyo, Jacob and Leandra, Jacob and Hyo, and Hyo and Leandra. Since you are their teacher, you could interact socially with each of your four students as well. So, for a class of four, there are actually 10 different paired combinations that exist in your classroom. We know, though, that classrooms regularly include more than four students;

the average class size is 20. So how many possible paired combinations exist in a class that size? Were you able to compute it mathematically? If you had, you would have found that there would be 190 paired combinations, and if you include yourself as their teacher in your calculations, it would total 210. That's a lot of possible paired combinations! Why is this important to know? As I mentioned previously, understanding paired combinations can illuminate the many possible social interactions that can exist in a classroom. This helps us to realize that classrooms have an overabundance of opportunities for students to socially interact.

Keep thinking!

K.

"Communication" is a conceptual word that requires carrying out many demonstrable social skills. Communication includes skills inherent to expression (talking, writing, and gesturing) and to reception (listening and processing). It also includes taking turns. As you probably already know, some students do well with the expressive part of communication but not so well with the receptive part. Others do better with the receptive and not so much with the expressive. And turn-taking, that can be hard for all students. The same is true for teachers. Teachers need to find a good balance with their expressive and receptive communication, and, just as important, they need to acquire the ability to facilitate students' development with doing so.

It is likely that some students will not come to your classroom as strong communicators, but you can help them become that way. Teachers can start to help students learn to communicate well by giving them plenty of practice with it. Teachers are not the only ones with information in the classroom; students have important experiences, knowledge, and skills that they can share with classmates. What they know can and will enhance other students' learning as well. Research has found that students who have opportunities to communicate with each other outperform those who did not have such experiences.

Dear future teacher,

Once when I was observing in a middle school classroom, I saw a gigantic sign posted on a wall that everyone could see. It said, "Ask 3 Before Me!" I must admit, my mind quickly wandered away from my observation as I thought about what those four words conveyed about the teacher who posted them. To me, it communicated something really grand—such as, even though I am your teacher, I know that I am not the only one who has answers to help you. There are many students in our class, and I trust that if you ask them, you will find someone who will help you learn.

Will you create such a sign for your students? I hope you do!

K.

There are many teaching strategies that include opportunities for students to learn from each other. Some strategies are rather informal, like "Ask 3 before me," but many are more formally structured. For example, I've seen some teachers skillfully implement peer tutoring in their classrooms by using student data to pair tutors with tutees. Sometimes, homogeneous groups were used, while at other times teachers implemented pairs with mixed abilities. Both arrangements have been found to offer all students favorable outcomes. Peer tutoring is most appealing because it promotes students' academic learning while simultaneously contributing to developing students' social skills—indeed, another win–win when facilitating students' academic and social emotional development. Research has shown that peer tutoring, at all grade levels can and will improve students' outcomes (Okilwa & Shelby, 2010; Mastropieri et al., 2007; Fuchs et al., 2000).

Teachers can promote student interaction in many ways; peer tutoring is just one of them. Another is cooperative learning. Sometimes I've heard teachers use the words "group work" and "cooperative learning" interchangeably, but the two strategies are not the same. There's a lot more to cooperative learning than gathering a small group of students together—I hope you recall it from Chapter 11. Cooperative learning is a teaching strategy that establishes an interdependence among all group members' tasks so everyone is needed to reach a shared goal (Johnson & Johnson, 1990; Slavin, 1994). Both peer tutoring and cooperative learning have the notion of interdependence at their core. The message conveyed to students when they experience interdependence may likely be this: It's good that I need you and you need me to work and learn together. It is important that we each do our part to reach our goal because we cannot reach it alone.

When students work together, it provides them with opportunities to become socially aware of ways their classmates are diverse and to recognize that others' opinions and perceptions may be very different than their own. Teachers can contribute to facilitating students' social awareness by talking about differences rather than ignoring them, by encouraging and teaching students to respectfully ask questions about diversity, and to be thoughtful and considerate with word choice.

It's important to help students develop the ability to listen to others. When they listen and understand others' circumstances, they can begin to develop a sense of compassion and empathy, which can help support and alleviate others' worries, concerns, and stress. If a student says to you, "I feel really excited about something," you probably have a good idea of what the student is feeling. At other times students' situations are uniquely their own and it will be especially important that you listen to what they are saying (and perhaps notice what they are not saying) to give you insight into how you might help. When emotions feel very strong and all-encompassing, when students' lives are full of events that can conjure up complex feelings that can be confusing to them, teachers can help by listening so students can make sense of their moods and reactions. Listening—what do you know about it?

Dear future teacher,

Early in my career, I was very involved with an organization called Landmark Education, a wonderful company that offers courses on personal and professional development. I heard about a course they offered called The Communications Course. The title alone caught my attention because I thought it could give me insight into how to polish my communication skills to effectively present information to others. I bet you can imagine my surprise when on the first day of the course, the instructor said, "well, I am sure many of you came to this course with a goal to work on your articulation and your speaking skills to portray your ideas to others." As he was talking, I nodded eagerly, "Yes! Exactly! This will be perfect," I thought. I sat up a little taller. And then he said, "well, this course will have nothing to do with those things. This is a course in communications and much of the power in communication resides in the listening, not in the speaking." I was flabbergasted. I wondered, "How could information about listening fill a 10-week course? I'll tell you, that 10-week experience was a game changer for me. The idea of each class was to learn how our listening can and will profoundly contribute to others. What a transformational experience it was!

How would you describe your capacity to truly listen to others?

K.

When students interact with each other, it naturally increases the chances conflicts will arise. It's important for students to know that is normal for conflicts to occasionally arise in any relationship, and everyone will experience them at times. While teachers don't have the power to make all of their students' conflicts go away, they do have the ability to help students learn how to manage, cope with, and resolve conflicts with care and respect.

Conflict resolution requires strong communication skills. It requires the ability to be self-aware and talk about emotions and behaviors, to listen to others' perspectives, and to have a desire to resolve the conflict itself. Conflict resolution can be hard work for everyone involved. It's not always easy for students to talk about emotions with others. It can make them feel vulnerable to talk about feelings. Some students will try to avoid it altogether. But students can learn how to work toward resolving conflicts because there is a lot of benefit in them doing so. Conflict resolution skills are an important component to social emotional learning.

Dear future teacher,

Conflict resolution can become part of all students' classrooms and schools. You may know of programs that encourage students to use a resolution plan, including using a protocol to establish ground rules, to decide who talks first, and to identify the roles each will take during the resolution process. Sometimes schools have effectively implemented peer mediators who offer students support using processes to resolve conflicts. Many conflict resolution programs have been found to be effective with students. I implemented a quite simple process that worked well. When I taught first grade, students often experienced conflicts that I believed they could learn to resolve themselves. While young children's conflicts may seem innocuous to us, I knew they were important to them. I wanted to support and encourage students to talk out their conflicts so I found some extra chairs and labeled them the Talking Chairs. I moved them to the side of the classroom to create a neutral meeting space for students who would use them. I introduced the ideas of the Talking Chairs to my students, and we worked together to come up with ground rules: One person talks at a time. Take turns talking. No one leaves until they say they are sorry for their role in what happened. Give a hug, a high five, or a handshake when you are finished. That was it. I spent some time modeling what it would look like and sound like when using the Talking Chairs by sitting in one myself and asking a student to sit in the chair across from me. Students watched and listened carefully. I told them that the purpose of the Talking Chairs was to talk out their problems. Students used them often. To help you understand the value and power of these chairs, I'll share an example of an observation I made.

One day, Allyson and Clarissa came in from recess and went right over and sat down in the Talking Chairs. I watched them, but since I was on the other side of our classroom, I couldn't hear what they were saying. It was time for math class to start. I looked over at Allyson and Clarissa. They were still in the Talking Chairs, but this time they were both crying while talking. I wondered if I should intervene, but I decided not to do so. I thought I should give them time to try to work through it. I let them talk longer, and eventually they stopped crying. I saw them get up and hug each other. Then they quietly walked to their own desks and sat down. I wouldn't have believed the power of the Talking Chairs if I hadn't seen it firsthand. When students have time and space to talk about their feelings and emotions, they have opportunities to develop empathy and compassion for others. They learn that there is great value in understanding someone else and that doing so creates a better world for everyone. Sometimes, all students need time and space to talk out their problems, and, in this case, the Talking Chairs worked very well.

Maybe you will have Talking Chairs in your classroom. I hope you do!

K.

Students make decisions every day. Teachers can help guide students toward developing responsible decision-making, which includes thinking about their actions and potential consequences for themselves and others impacted by the decisions made. Teachers can encourage students to remember that they are not alone, and while they can become strong as individuals (and we hope they do), they can become even stronger when they are part of a caring community. Students' social and emotional learning matters, and teachers can play an important role in facilitating its development. The touchstone for this chapter is: **Students' social and emotional development will provide a strong foundation for their academic learning** (Goleman, 1995).

TOUCHSTONE FOR TEACHING: STUDENTS' SOCIAL AND EMOTIONAL DEVELOPMENT WILL PROVIDE A STRONG FOUNDATION FOR THEIR ACADEMIC LEARNING

What to Do	What Not to Do
Provide opportunities for students to talk with peers about academic and social topics. Students need to be able to make sense of their ideas by talking with each other.	Don't talk over students. They need time to express their thoughts and emotions.
Encourage students to develop a self-awareness of their emotions. They will need time to identify the feelings they have.	Don't assume that students are aware of the feelings they have. Some may not know.
Create a safe space for students to talk about their emotions. Students need to feel a sense of safety and trust when talking about emotions.	Don't presume students will be willing to talk about their feelings anywhere. They often need a safe space to feel comfortable doing so.
Find ways to embed social emotional learning into daily lessons and curriculum. Strive to embed social and emotional development in academic lessons.	Don't think that there's not enough time in the school day to include social and emotional learning. It can be embedded naturally into many moments within what you already do.
Encourage students to participate in conflict resolution. They can learn to independently solve many of their own problems.	Don't assume that students can solve all of their own problems. Teachers' guidance can help a lot.

Questions for Discussion and Reflection

- How do you feel about discussing your feelings and emotions with others? How do you feel when others do so with you?
- Why is academic learning impacted by students' emotional well-being? Please write a short scenario as an example that supports your response.
- What are some intrapersonal and interpersonal skills teachers can help students develop? How can teachers help to develop them?
- What are Talking Chairs, and how could they be helpful with implementing conflict resolution?

PART 6

Why We Teach

CHAPTER 14

TEACHING AS AN ACT OF ADVOCACY

I believe all would agree that all students deserve to have every opportunity to reach their fullest potential so they can make the best of their lives and experience true individual satisfaction and fulfillment. There are times when all students need adults to advocate for them along the way, to be on their side and speak on their behalf, to stand up for what's best for them as they grow and mature. While we know that self-advocacy is important, students—especially our youngest and most vulnerable—do not always have a voice that is powerful enough to ask for what they need and to make a change that would help them along the way. It takes adults who are in students' lives to be willing to voice their opinions and call for change when they see it's needed. Teachers can play an important role in serving in that capacity for their students.

Maybe you've heard the saying "Teaching is a work of heart!" I believe that it's true. Teachers care deeply for their students and are invested in doing the best they can to meet all of their needs. Teacher advocacy can begin right where they are—in their classrooms—by making a difference with what they say and do. In what ways could teachers' practices serve as acts of advocacy? The answer resides in teachers critically examining their teaching practices and purposefully talking about and educating their students, faculty members, and others about their concerns, intentions, and actions.

While teacher advocacy can and will benefit all students, undoubtedly students who are from historically marginalized groups, including those who been excluded due to their race, class, gender, ability, language, religion, or sexual orientation would benefit from teachers' conscious advocacy in what they say and what they do. Teachers can be changemakers—and when it comes to their students, there's a lot they can do to make difference.

Teachers can be advocates for their students when creating a classroom environment where all students feel and are emotionally and physically safe and productive. Classrooms need to be emotionally safe places where students feel comfortable sharing ideas aloud. Classrooms are emotionally safe when they are free from put-downs, bias, and exclusion. While many teachers will consciously work toward creating a classroom community such as this, the difference with teacher advocates is that they explain to others why emotionally safe spaces contribute to all students' learning. They teach students and other teachers why advocacy is important and how it can help students who are susceptible to not feeling safe. We know all too well that some students can be easy targets for name calling, put-downs, and bullying, and teachers can do a lot to set guidelines in their classrooms to ensure that doesn't happen.

Teachers have a lot of autonomy to design the physical layout of their classrooms, and some considerations that can be made when advocating for spaces that work well for students. This is especially important for students with physical disabilities. Classrooms need to be spaces where students can safely and comfortably move about, whether it's to "run, walk, ride, or roll" through classroom doors. Teachers can talk openly about this need to students and to other teachers. They can advocate for students by asking for different desks or seating and ensuring school hallways are easily accessible. Some schools can be hard to navigate, with ramps, steps, carpets, and tile. Teachers can talk with students to come up with ways to ensure all students can move through all spaces easily. It can be as simple as, "We need Natasha to be able to move around easily in her wheelchair. Let's take a close look at our classroom and school to see what we can do to make it safe and easy for her to move through." From my experiences, students enjoy being included to solve a real-world problem like this, and they can contribute in meaningful and worthwhile ways. A bonus is that this collaboration can often draw all students closer together while helping Natasha feel important and fully included in the classroom.

It is important for teachers to consider language use when advocating for students. Teachers' language creates a classroom tone and culture that is a very real and influential part of students' environments. Teachers who are advocates for students are highly conscious and selective with their word choice and have high expectations for their students to have the same consideration. Teachers' words can be powerful—they can build students up as superheroes or shroud them with discouragement. Teachers can help students learn about word choice and ensure they use it respectfully when referring to students from historically marginalized groups.

Dear future teacher,

Students are not always aware that what they say can be hurtful to others. Often without much contemplation, students have used words that portray students with disabilities in very negative ways. I've heard students call others the R-word and mimic gestures that are meant to portray autism by using sarcastic behaviors. These words and actions are hurtful to the students with disabilities and to others who see and hear them. You may have heard about a wonderful advocacy group, Spread the Word to End the Word, which is a call given especially to students to pledge not use the R-word ever again. The last time I checked, the R-word campaign had over 800,000 online pledges from more than 6,000 schools in over 80 countries (spreadtheword.global). This is one small example of advocacy that is making a change.

Will you take the pledge? Will you encourage you students to do so too? I hope you do!

K.

Teachers can and should teach students about words to use that portray respectful ways to refer to racial groups. While racial vocabulary has changed and shifted over time, teachers can advocate for respectful language when referring to students of color, Black, Brown, biracial, multiracial, Asian, Latina, Latino, Latinx, and Native American, to name a few. Some students of color may not be as selective about the terminology that is used when talking about their race, but most will be, and it is important to talk openly about this with them, to respectfully ask about how they describe their individual identities. Making assumptions or generalizations will not help, and asking shows respect for everyone involved. All students can learn how to talk about racial differences, and when they learn to do so, they can become advocates by teaching others as well.

Teachers can also do a lot to encourage students not to use insensitive and offensive language on topics other than race too. For example, it can be common to hear students use phrases such as "that's so gay" and "you're so queer." These phrases are hurtful, especially to homosexual students, because these words include references to people who are gay and are meant to describe something that is perceived as wrong and weird. When phrases such as these are used for name-calling, it passes along a message that gay people are weird and wrong. Instead of ignoring statements like this, teachers can be advocates by interrupting the language to explain why it's hurtful and why is shouldn't be repeated. All students can be and should be taught not to use offensive and hurtful language.

Dear future teacher,

I'd like to tell you about GLSEN, the Gay, Lesbian, Straight Educators' Network, which is a teacher activist group that works toward "ensuring that every member of every school community is valued and respected regardless of sexual orientation, gender identity or gender expression" (GLSEN, 2019). The organization advocates for and helps to carry out policies to protect our LGBTQ youth. It has active chapters in 30 states throughout our nation. GLSEN currently has over 1.5 million students, parents, teachers, and allies working toward creating safe and affirming schools for all students. Our LGBTQ youth need teacher allies to be advocates for them, to encourage them to be fully themselves and to promote attitudes of tolerance and acceptance to others.

K.

Teachers who are advocates also carefully select their language when talking about gender differences as well. While we know that classrooms will include males and females, we also know that gender is not binary. Transgender students deserve and need to have language used that is supportive and inclusive of them. It's important for teachers not to refer to their classes as "Boys and Girls," for example, but to use more inclusive language instead. It is also important for teachers to ask transgender students the names and pronouns that align best with their identities. Since ideas such as this may be new to some students, teachers can teach about transgender identities and how to be allies and supports for transgender people.

Dear future teacher,

It is imperative that teachers support all students' identities and encourage students to be fully who they are. Have you heard of the Human Rights Campaign (HRC)? They are a wonderful organization focused on advocating for lesbian, gay, bisexual, transgender, and queer (LGBTQ) people's rights. They have more than three million members and supporters who align with their work to provide support to work for equality for the LGBTQ community. The HRC recently reported that "41% of all transgender students have attempted suicide at some point in their lives" (HRC, 2018). The HRC also reported that transgender young people regularly experience rejection, bullying, and harassment "just for being who they are" (HRC, 2018). Teacher advocates can work toward changing these experiences for transgender students by openly discussing and teaching about the importance of fully respecting those who are transgender and all students who identify as part of the LGBTQ community.

What can you do to help?

K.

Teachers and their curriculum go hand in hand. Teachers follow the curriculum to determine what is taught to students, and they often have say in its adjustment. Teachers who are advocates can critically examine the curriculum to ensure the content is presented accurately, and just as important, critically analyze it to ensure all cultures and races are represented. Howard Zinn, author of *A People's History of the United States* (2005), disclosed a whole new reality when he rewrote the history of the United States by portraying it from underrepresented voices, including women, Native Americans, those in poverty, people of color, and immigrants. Zinn's work echoed a movement to critically examine ways that a dominant voice is often heard over others, a voice that promotes and perpetuates oppression, that of the White, Christian, heterosexual, English-speaking, able-bodied male. Teachers who are advocates for underrepresented people have worked hard to rewrite and reteach stories from other perspectives as a way to teach for social justice. All teachers can use curriculum materials that are antibias and free from stereotyping and prejudice to work toward ensuring that all voices and perspectives are represented in the curriculum.

Teachers have plenty of opportunities to be highly selective with the materials they use. To promote outcomes of historically marginalized students, resources need to be free from bias and stereotypes and represent the diversity of students using them. While critically examining instructional materials and resources can seem like an additional, time-consuming task, there are many organizations that provide this service free to teachers; the materials are easily located and widely available. Organizations such as Learning for Justice, Teaching for Change, and the National Education Association's Ed Justice provide lists of resources and services that teacher–advocates can use to promote antibias education and teaching for social justice.

Teaching materials can include subtle messages that perpetuate gender bias as well. Materials that portray males completing activities and achievements more often than females can be discouraging and lessen the motivation for females to learn. While research shows that gender bias is seen to a lesser degree throughout the past few decades, many researchers suggest that the general curriculum is still gender biased (Sadker et al., 2009).

Dear future teacher,

Sexism is a real part of our society and of our schools, and a lot can be done in classrooms to work toward eliminating it. The first step toward providing equal opportunities for female and male classmates is to understand the prevalent concerns that exist. The attention teachers give to students plays an important role in students' interest and achievement. Research has suggested that although gender inequality is improving in schools, teachers can still give males up to two thirds more attention than females (Sadker et al., 2009). Being aware of this disparity is the first step. Working toward balancing this during instruction is the second. Teachers can work toward balancing their attention, questions, focus, discussions, and responses to help eliminate gender bias in their instruction. They can teach students about the concerns of sexism, which can contribute to providing females with more opportunities for success. Creating a truly antibias classroom takes deliberate introspection and reflection, worthwhile effort to make learning experiences equitable for all students.

K.

One of the most discouraging statistics reported is that more than 10 million children in the United States are currently living in poverty. The childhood poverty rate is nearly 15%. This means that for a family of four, their annual income would be at or below $26,000 or roughly $2,000 a month (Children's Defense Fund, 2022). When children live in poverty, they experience consequences that do not originate from their own actions. They can encounter the harmful and often irreversible effects of hunger and malnutrition, including cognitive and physical disabilities and mental health issues. They often experience unhealthy housing or homelessness, which can contribute to increased stress and lead to drug use and addiction. Students living in poverty have increased school absenteeism and dropout rates. It is additionally troubling that nearly 73% of children living in poverty are children of color (Children's Defense Fund, 2020). It is important for all teachers to know that students who live in poverty have many challenges associated with food scarcity, housing concerns, and health care issues. Teachers who are advocates can take time to know families' needs and to provide information about services and resources that could help to improve their situation. Teachers can also learn about classism to understand the bias, prejudice, and discrimination that comes from believing people from one class are better than another. They can work toward creating a classroom environment that is supportive of students living in poverty. Doing so will help to build equitable opportunities for learning.

Historically, our students of color—especially those who identify as Black and Brown—have repeatedly underperformed their classmates. While the causes of this achievement-gap are systemic, originating from complex racial issues inherent to our larger society, teachers have been working in many ways to eliminate the negative effects of racial bias, racial stereotyping, and racial prejudice from their classrooms and schools. Teachers who provide opportunities for students to talk about racial differences openly, that teach how to be anti racist and provide lessons about race-related vocabulary, portray anti racist activism during their instruction. Students spend at least 13 years of their lives in school, which offers a lot of time to learn how to reduce and eliminate racial bias, prejudice, and discrimination from classrooms, schools, and our society. Teachers who are advocates for racial equality promote anti racist teaching practices by openly talking about these ideas with their students, co-teachers, and community. They work toward knowing their own identities and identifying and eliminating their own conscious and unconscious bias. They work toward developing a resilient anti racist, multicultural consciousness and find ways to demonstrative their acceptance, respect, and appreciation for racial diversity and racial self-expression.

Dear future teacher,

Our world is a different place after the wrongful deaths of George Floyd and Breonna Taylor. Their deaths illuminated the racial inequalities, mistreatment, and injustice we have all lived with for far too long. People throughout our nation and world have joined the Black Lives Matter social movement, an activist group focused on bringing "justice, healing and freedom" to all Black people. One of my students talked with me about the Black Lives Matter movement and his response was, "To me, ALL lives matter." I took time to explain to him and my other students that when we say, Black Lives Matter, it does not mean that only Black lives matter; it means that Black lives deserve the time and attention to be noticed NOW. If we were to quickly replace the phrase Black Lives Matter with All Lives Matter, it would replicate the problem that has continued to exist and persist for generations—that of Black lives have been oppressed, kept down, and restrained. Black Lives Matter at School is an advocacy group that extends the Black Lives Matter movement into school settings. The organization provides curriculum and resources for educators and students to work toward racial justice and equality and to end racism. The Black Lives Matter at School provides important resources to help become a strong teacher–advocate for Black students. Our Black student need all teachers' advocacy.

How can you help?

K.

It is essential that we work together to help all students succeed and that we are consistently conscious of uplifting students who have been historically marginalized and have historically underperformed in our schools and classrooms. Someone once said to me, "It is not our differences that separate us. It is our attitudes about differences that keep us apart." Isn't that true? The goal of all teachers is to help all students, every single one of them, reach their fullest potential. Students will not be able to do that if the barriers of racism, classism, sexism, ableism, anti-Semitism, and homophobia continue to block their paths. All "isms" need not exist. They are only alive because of the perceptions, beliefs, and opinions that give life to them. It's important that we all join together to work toward reaching a shared goal, where all of our students—every single one of them—are perceived as equally worthwhile, equally whole and complete, equally significant in our schools, classrooms, and the world in which we live.

All students need advocates, those who provide an unwavering support for them. Chapter 14 suggests that classroom teachers can and need to serve as daily advocates for their students and families. The touchstone for this chapter is:

Advocating for students will contribute to their social, emotional, and academic development (Ridnouer, 2011).

TOUCHSTONE FOR TEACHING: ADVOCATING FOR STUDENTS WILL CONTRIBUTE TO THEIR SOCIAL, EMOTIONAL, AND ACADEMIC DEVELOPMENT

What to Do	What Not to Do
Listen to students to identify their needs and talk about their needs with others who can help.	Don't assume that students' needs will be known by others. They will often need to hear it explained.
Strive to carry out advocacy in your own classroom.	Don't wait for others to organize movements to make a change. It can begin with you.
Take action to make changes that can promote students' well-being and growth. Teach students about the importance of being self-advocates and advocates for others.	Don't think your voice and actions won't make a difference. If needed, you alone can advocate for students' needs.
Encourage students to make changes in their school and in the world so it is a better place for everyone.	Don't think that adults are the only ones who can carry out advocacy work. Students of all ages have powerful ideas that can lead to important changes in our world.

Questions for Discussion and Reflection

- Why is it important for teachers to be advocates for their students? What would it look like? What would it sound like?
- This chapter introduces the concept of advocacy starting with the language and word choices teachers use. What examples from the chapter do you find important? In what ways are teacher language and student advocacy connected?
- Describe what the following quote means to you: "It's not our differences that separate us. It's our attitudes about differences that keep us apart."
- In what ways could you be an advocate for children? What topic would be your focus? What would you say? What would you do?
- Why is it important for teachers to be advocates for students? In what ways could teacher advocacy lead to improved student outcomes?

Fig. 14.1. Copyright © 2015 Depositphotos/Wavebreakmedia.

CHAPTER 15

CONTRIBUTING TO THE TEACHING PROFESSION

Dear future teacher,

There have been many changes in the field of education through-out the past decade. We've seen student demographics change considerably; our schools have seen an increase in students of color, English language learners, students living in poverty, and students with disabilities being educated in general education classrooms. We've seen dramatic shifts in teaching materials from blackboards to whiteboards to online applications. And we've seen different schooling options become available for families, including more magnet and charter schools. But nothing has impacted the field of education more than the COVID—19 pandemic that immediately interrupted schooling for all students across our nation beginning in spring 2020. Schools shut down and nearly instantaneously, teachers had to shift their in-person instruction to online platforms. Questions surfaced that needed immediate answers, including which students have technology available at home that can be used to access lessons? Do all students have access to the internet? How can students have access to learning materials? These questions are about access, the ability to enter, and technology and the internet became the classroom doors for students, their teachers, and their learning. COVID—19 illuminated the already prevalent concerns for students of economically challenged families. Teachers and community members worked hard to solve issues surrounding access. In some cases, laptops and other electronic devices were provided to families so students could participate in distance learning, and in other instances where the internet was not available, teachers and school personnel delivered learning materials to students, in many cases door-to-door. Teachers across our nation worked day and night to find ways to connect with their students to ensure learning would continue and to reassure their students that they were concerned about and cared for.

The effects of COVID—19 on students' health have been significant and have impacted their attendance in school. In November 2020, The American Pediatrics Association reported that over one million children in the United States—infants, youth, and teens—had tested positive for the virus. In addition, students across our nation were regularly in isolation and quarantine due to family members, classmates, and friends contracting the virus. When students' schooling is interrupted, their learning is also interrupted. In addition to student attendance, teachers have had to grapple with tough challenges that were outside of their control, including unavailable or nonworking internet connections, unavailable electronic devices, nonworking electronic devices, unavailable learning materials, and home environments not conducive to students' online learning. Once these issues are addressed, and certainly not all could or will ever be, even larger challenges surface: "what can teachers do to promote students' learning in online platforms?" It goes without saying that countless new online applications become available every day to promote students' learning. Teachers regularly seek and sort through them in an effort to find ways to best help their students learn. Options abound, including different learning platforms (virtual spaces for streamlining teaching and learning online), different mixed media (images, video, audio, animation, and text), and a variety of different social media (virtual applications to promote social interaction). All these options are online teaching tools, and today's teachers have been pioneers as they've plowed through the incalculable options available to them. Indeed, they have worked long and hard to find what's worked well for their students. I taught during the time of the pandemic and experienced all of this. Once settled into teaching online, it's become apparent that the touchstones presented in this book remain applicable to virtual teaching as well. That is because teaching is about relating to students, facilitating their learning, and helping all students reach their highest potential. The touchstones remain as universal reference points that can be used when teaching in person or in online learning environments because each identifies and describes what students need from teachers in order to succeed.

Our students need teachers who are committed to the teaching profession. We need teachers who are dedicated to contributing to the holistic wellness of their students, to creating inclusive and productive learning environments, to promoting a welcoming and caring learning climate and culture in schools that will contribute to our larger communities. Our students are waiting, and our profession is ready to widen our circle for you. Please come.

With my warmest regards,

K.

REFERENCES

Albert, L. (2002). *Cooperative discipline.* AGS Publishing.

Aronson, B. & Laughter, J. (2016). The theory and practice of culturally relevant education: A synthesis of the research across content areas. *Review of Educational Research, 86*(1), 163–206.

Almeida, J., Johnson, R.M., Corliss, H.L., Molner, B.E. & Azrael, D. (2009). Emotional distress among LGBT youth: The influence of perceived discrimination based on sexual orientation. *Journal of Youth and Adolescence, 38*(7), 1001–10014.

Ayscue, J. & Siegel-Hawley, G. (2019). Magnets and school turnarounds: Revisiting policies for promoting equitable, diverse schools. *Education Policy Analysis Archives, 27*(72), 1–38.

Berkowitz, R., Moore, H., Astor, R. A., & Benbenishty, R. (2017). A research synthesis of the associations between socioeconomic background, inequality, school climate, and academic achievement. *Review of Educational Research, 87*(2). 425–469.

Bethell, C. D., Newacheck, P., Hawes, E., & Halfon, N. (2014). Adverse childhood experiences: Assessing the impact on health and school engagement and the mitigating role of resilience. *Health Affairs, 33*(12), 2106– 2115.

Brown, E. (2016, January 20). Rats, roaches, mold—poor conditions lead to teacher sickout, closure for most Detroit schools. *The Washington Post.* https://www.washingtonpost.com/news/education/wp/2016/01/20/rats-roaches-mold-poor-conditions-leads-to-teacher-sickout-closure-of-most-detroit-schools/

Brownlee, K., Rawana, E., & MacArthur, J. (2012). Implementation of a strengths-based approach to teaching in an elementary school. *Journal of Teaching and Learning, 8*(1), 1–12.

CAST (2023). *About Universal Design for Learning.* CAST. https://www.cast.org/impact/universal-design-for-learning-udl

Cataldi, E. F., Laird, J., & KewalRamani, A. (2009). High school dropout and completion rates in the United States: 2007 (NCES 2009-064). National Center for Education Statistics, Institute of Education Sciences, U.S. Department of Education, Washington, D.C. https://nces.ed.gov/pubsearch/pubsinfo.asp?pubid=2009064 Centers for Disease Control and Prevention. Annual Report. (September, 2016). https://www.cdc.gov/globalhealth/resources/reports/annual/pdf/CGH_Annual-Report_2016.pdf

Children and Nature Network. (2022). https://www.childrenandnature.org/

Children's Defense Fund, (2020). https://www.childrensdefense.org/

Children's Defense Fund, (2022). The state of America's children 2021. https://www.childrensdefense.org/state-of-americas-children/soac-2021-child-poverty/

Cochran-Smith, M. (2004). *Walking the road: Race, diversity, and social justice in teacher education.* Teachers College Press.

Collaborative for Academic, Social, and Emotional Learning (CASEL). (2021). https://casel.org

Cook, G. (2015). Responding to student trauma. *Education Update, 57*(12), 2-6.

Crosby, S., Somers, C., Day, A., Zammit, M. Shier, J., & Baroni, B. (2017). Examining school attachment, social support, and trauma symptomatology among court-involved, female students. *Journal of Child and Family Studies, 26,* 2539–2546.

Delpit, L. (1995). *Other people's children: Cultural conflict in the classroom.* New Press.

Delpit, L. (2013). Educators as "seed people" growing a new future. *Educational Researcher, 7*(32), 14–21.

Derman-Sparks, L., & Edwards, J. O. (2010). *Anti-bias education for young children and ourselves.* National Association for the Education of Young Children.

DeRobertis, E. (2010). Deriving a third force approach to child development from the works of Alfred Adler. *Journal of Humanistic Psychology, 51*(4), 492–515.

Dewey, J. (1963). *Experience and education.* The Kappa Delta Pi Lecture Series. Macmillan.

Dover, A. (2009). Teaching for social justice and K-12 student outcomes: A conceptual framework and research review. *Equity and Excellence in Education, 42*(4), 506–524.

Drummond, S., & Kamenetz, A. (2014, September 2). *The end of neighborhood schools.* NPR. https://apps.npr.org/the-end-of-neighborhood-schools/

Duncombe, W., & Yinger, J. (2004). How much more does a disadvantaged student cost? *Center for Policy Research, 103.* https://surface.syr.edu/cpr/103

Epstein, J. L. (1991). Effects of student achievement of teachers' practices of parent involvement. In S. B. Silvern (Ed.). *Advances in reading/language research: A research annual, Vol. 5. Literacy through family, community and school interaction* (pp. 261-276). Elsevier Science: JAI Press.

Every Student Succeeds Act, 20 U.S.C. § 6310 (2015). https://www.congress.gov/bill/114th-congress/senate-bill/1177

Fraser, B. (1991). Two decades of classroom environment research. In B.J. Fraser & H. J. Walberg (Eds.), *Educational environments: Evaluation, antecedents and consequences* (pp. 3–27). Pergamon Press.

Fuchs, D., Fuchs, L., & Burish, P. (2000). Peer-assisted learning strategies: An evidence-based practice to promote reading achievement. *Learning Disabilities Research and Practice, 15*(2), 85–91.

Gains, K., & Curry, Z. (2011). The inclusive classroom: The effects of color on learning and behavior. *Journal of family and consumer sciences education, 29*(1), 56–57.

Gay and Lesbian Straight Educators Network (GLSEN), (2019). https://glsen.org

Goddard, Y., Goddard, R., & Tschannen-Moran, M. (2007). A theoretical and empirical investigation of teacher collaboration for school improvement and student achievement in public elementary schools. *Teacher College Record, 109*(4), 877–896.

Goldberg, G., & Houser, R. (2017, July 19). *Battling decision fatigue.* Edutopia. https://www.edutopia.org/blog/battling-decision-fatigue-gravity-goldberg-renee-houser

Goleman, D. (1995). *Emotional intelligence.* Bantam Books.

Goodlad, J. (1984). *A place called school: Prospects for the future.* McGraw-Hill.

Grammer, R. (1986). See me beautiful [Song]. *On Teaching Peace* [Album]. Smilin' Atcha Music, Inc.

Griffith, D. (2019, October). Everybody's talking about the whole child. *Educational Leadership*, 90–91.

Henderson, A., Mapp, K., Johnson, V., & Davies, D. (2007). *Beyond the bake sale: The essential guide to family–school partnerships*. New Press.

Heschong Mahone Group. (1999). *Daylighting in schools: An investigation into the relationship between daylighting and human performance*. https://h-m-g.com/downloads/Daylighting/schoolc.pdf

Human Rights Campaign. (2018). 2018 *LGBTQ Youth Report*. https://www.hrc.org/resources/2018-lgbtq-youth-report

Jennings, P. (2019, Summer). Teaching in a trauma-sensitive classroom: What educators can do to support students. *American Educator*, 12–43.

Jimenez, T., Graf, V., & Rose, E. (2007). Gaining access to general education: The promise of universal design for learning. *Issues in Teacher Education, 16*(2). 41–54.

Johnson, D. W., & Johnson, R. T. (1990). Cooperative learning and achievement. In S. Sharan (Ed.), *Cooperative Learning: Theory and Research* (pp. 23–37). Praeger.

Johnson, D. W., & Johnson, R. T. (2009). An educational psychology success story: Social interdependence theory and cooperative learning. *Educational Researcher, 38*(5), 365–379.

Kinnealey, M., Pfeiffer, B., Miller, J., & Roan, C. (2012). Effect of classroom modification on attention and engagement of students with autism or dyspraxia. *American Journal of Occupational Therapy, 66*, 511–519.

Klein, A. (2021, December 6). 1500 decisions a day (At least!): How teachers cope with a dizzying array of questions. *Education Week*: https://www.edweek.org/teaching-learning/1-500-decisions-a-day-at-least-how-teachers-cope-with-a-dizzying-array-of-questions/2021/12?utm_source=nl&utm_medium=eml&utm_campaign=eu&M=64237396&U=1332932&UUID=7a5a250d6c3b344aa829ea733f3fc086

Kohn, A. (2006). *Beyond discipline: From compliance to community* (10th edition). Alexandra, VA: ASCD.

Kohn, A. (1995). Discipline is the problem—not the solution. *Learning Magazine*. https://www.alfiekohn.org/article/discipline-problem-solution/

Ladson-Billings, G. (1995). But that's just good teaching! The case for culturally relevant pedagogy. *Theory into Practice, 34*(3). 159–165.

Larocque, M., Kleinman, I., & Darling, S. (2011). Parental involvement: The missing link in school achievement. *Preventing School Failure, 55*(3), 115–122.

Learning for Justice. (1997). Starting small: Teaching children tolerance in preschool and the early grades. Learning for Justice. https://www.learningforjustice.org/classroom-resources/film-kits/starting-small

Learning for Justice. (2022). https://learningforjustice.org

Lundeberg, M. A. (1997). You guys are overreacting: Teaching prospective teachers about subtle gender bias. *Journal of Teacher Education, 48(*1), 55–60.

Mahnke, F. H. (1996). *Color, environment, and human response: An interdisciplinary understanding of color and its use as a beneficial element in the design of the architectural environment*. Van Nostrand Reinhold, 1–234.

Malaguzzi, L. (1998). History, ideas and basic philosophy: An interview with Leila Gandini. In C. Edwards, L. Gandini & G. Forman (Eds.) *The hundred languages of children* (pp. 49–97). Ablex.

Marzano, R. (1992). *A different kind of learning: Teaching with dimensions of learning*. Association of Supervision and Curriculum Development.

Mastropieri, M. A., Scruggs, T. E., & Berkeley, S. L. (2007, February). Peers helping peers. *Educational Leadership,* 54–58.

McFarland, J., Hussar, B., Zhang, J., Wang, X., Wang, K., Hein, S., Diliberti, M., Forrest Cataldi, E., Bullock Mann, F., & Barmer, A. (2019). *The condition of education 2019. (NCES 2019–144).* U.S. Department of Education. National Center for Education Statistics. https://nces.ed.gov/pubsearch/pubsinfo.asp?pubid=2019144

McQuiggan, M., & Megra, M. (2017). *Parent and family involvement in education: Results from the national household education surveys program of 2016 (NCES, 2017–102).* U.S. Department of Education. National Center for Education Statistics. http://nces. ed.gov/pubsearch/pubsinfo.asp?pubid=2017102

National Association for Multicultural Education (NAME). (2019). https://nameorg.org

Neito, S. (2009). *Language, culture and teaching: Critical perspectives.* Routledge.

Noddings, N. (2005). *Caring in education.* Infed. https://www.uvm.edu/~rgriffin/ NoddingsCaring.pdf

No Child Left Behind (NCLB) Act of 2001, 20 U.S. C. § 6319 (2002).

Oblack, R. (2019). *Back-to-school after hurricane katrina: The New Orleans school district makes changes and adjustments.* Thought Co. https://www.thoughtco.com/ back-to-school-after-hurricane-katrina-3443854

Okilwa, N. S. A., & Shelby, L. (2010). The effects of peer tutoring on students' academic performance of students with disabilities in grades 6–12: A synthesis of the literature. *Remedial and Special Education, 31*(6). 450– 463.

Perry, B. D. (2005). Maltreatment and the developing child: How early childhood exposure shapes child and culture. The Margaret McCain Lecture Series. https://www. lfcc.on.ca/mccain/perry.pdf

Ridnouer, K. (2011). *Everyday engagement: Making students and parents your partners in learning.* ASCD.

Ronfeldt, M., Farmer, S. O., McQueen, K., & Grossom, J. (2015). Teacher collaboration in instructional teams and student achievement. *American Educational Research Journal.* https://journals.sagepub.com/doi/full/10.3102/0002831215585562

Rosenthal, R., & Babad, E. (1985). Pygmalion in the gymnasium. *Educational Leadership, 43*(1), 36-39.

Rosenthal, R., & Jacobson, L. (1968). Teacher expectations for the disadvantaged. *Scientific American, 218*(4), 19–23.

Rosenthal, R., & Rubin, D. B. (1978). Interpersonal expectancy effects: The first 345 studies. *Behavioral and Brain Sciences, 1*(3), 377–415.

Sadker, D. M., Sadker, M. P., & Littleman, K. R. (2009). *Still failing at fairness: How gender bias cheats girls and boys in school and what we can do about it.* Scribner.

Sanchez, R. (2016, January 28). Detroit public schools hit with lawsuit. CNN. https://www. cnn.com/2016/01/28/us/detroit-public-schools-lawsuit/index.html

Sapon-Shevin, M. (1999). *Because we can change the world: A practical guide to building cooperative, inclusive classrooms.* Allyn & Bacon.

Seligman, M. E., Ernst, R. M., Gillham, J., Reivich, K., & Linkens, M. (2009). Positive education: positive psychology and classroom interventions. *Oxford Review of Education, 35*(3), 293–311.

Sensoy, O., & DiAngelo, R. (2009). Developing social justice literacy: An open letter to our faculty colleagues. *Phi Delta Kappan, 90*(5), 345–352.

Slade, S., & Griffith, D. (2013). A whole child approach to student success. *KEDI Journal of Educational Policy, 10*(3). 21–35.

Slavin, R. (1994). Quality, appropriateness, incentive, and time: A model of instructional effectiveness. *International Journal of Educational Research, 21*(2), 141–157.

Sorrell, M. E. (2019). Perceptions of flexible seating. *The Journal of Teacher Action Research, 5*(2), 120–136.

Staats, C. (2015, Winter). Understanding implicit bias: What educators should know. *American Educator, 29*–43.

Stronge, J. H. (2002). *Qualities of effective teachers.* ASCD.

Style, E. (1988). *Curriculum and window and mirror.* Listening for All Voices, Oak Knoll School monograph, Summit, NJ.

Sylwester, R. (1994). How emotions affect learning. *Educational Leadership, 52*(2), 60–65.

The Aspen Institute National Commission on Social, Emotional and Academic Development (2019). From a nation at risk to a nation at hope: Recommendations from the national commission on social, emotional and academic development. http://nationathope.org/

The National Traumatic Stress Network. (2021). https://nctsn.org

UDL in the ESSA. (2016, February 17). CAST. https://www.cast.org/news/2016/udl-in-the-essa

U.S. National Commission on Excellence in Education (1983). *A nation at risk: The imperative for educational reform: A report to the Nation and the Secretary of Education, U. S. Department of Education.* National Commission on Excellence in Education [Superintendent of Documents, U.S. Government Printing Office distributor].

Walberg, B. J. (1974). Classroom learning environments and effective schooling. *Professional School Psychology, 2*(1), 25–41.

Walker, T. (2019, May 29). *How closing schools traumatizes students and communities.* National Education Association. https://www.nea.org/advocating-for-change/new-from-nea/how-closing-schools-traumatizes-students-and-communities

Zakrzewski, V. S. (2012). Four ways teachers can show they care. *Greater Good Magazine.* https://greatergood.berkeley.edu/article/item/caring_teacher_student_relationship

Zinn, H. (2005). *A people's history of the United States.* Harper Perennial Modern Classics.